LIVING LIFE AS A SACRED PRACTICE

Discover Yourself as a Source of Creation

SHARON PARRIS-CHAMBERS

Contents

VALUES To Live By

Spiritual Development

Acknowledgements

The following persons and organizations are acknowledged
for their contributions and inspiration:

Wayne Dyer, PhD., Counseling Psychologist, Author
Sadhguru, Mystic & Founder Isha Foundation
Theo Chambers, Co-founder, Temple of Inner Peace

. . .

Special thanks to Amina Diop my daughter and Theo Chambers,
my husband for their unwavering support and encouragement.

Foreword

When Sharon asked me to be part of 'Living Life as a Sacred Practice,' her groundbreaking undertaking, I paused. What an honor, but respectfully, I asked for a day or two for reflection. I accepted, satisfied that I measured up ethically to the trust placed in me.

Sharon is a friend, in many respects, my soul friend - my Anam Cara - a term used by the Gaels to define their village confidante or confessor.

I have known Sharon for a decade and throughout, she has never wavered in her commitment to exploring philosophical truths and justice.

There's a magic, a transcendence, an authenticity to Sharon that eludes many in the field of wellness.

It is no secret that self-styled gurus have preyed upon the unsuspecting, the vulnerable and the neophyte. For sure, the purported road to the promise land is littered with charred psyches and disillusionment.

Weighed down by a relentlessly unforgiving fast-paced lifestyle, the soul cries out for restoration, for meaning, for eternal validity.

New Age Thought has responded, becoming the new Zeitgeist, the new reality. But what began as a genuine attempt to heal the psychically and emotionally wounded is now marred by commercialism and downright duplicity, hubris and prevarications.

The genuine master is a gem, a rare find - a breath of fresh air amid a palpable stench.

Sharon is that master. She expresses gratitude to her ancestors and elders for instructing her on life's meaning and the ways of nature.

In the book's 'Vignette,' she shares: "Leaving Kingston to visit with my grandparents in the rural part of Jamaica, cradled in the valley of the awesome Blue Mountains over 7,000 feet high, brought me in contact with my extended family - aunts, uncles and cousins. It strengthened my sense of responsibility…Most of all, it ignited in me the desire to explore my own true Divine nature and connection to the earth."

Her 2012 return to her roots in Gambia unveiled her calling and sealed her mission as a veritable messenger of Spirit. It is in Gambia that she was grounded and initiated into the innermost mystery. It is there that she drank from the well of the First People and was handed the fabled Philosopher's Stone.

No one can claim mastery without having returned to existence at its very embryonic, life-sustaining phase. Sharon returned to the village of Kinali. It was there that she received one of many initiations. She was handed the proverbial scepter from the elders, a symbol of authority as teacher and mystic. Her extended sojourn in Kinali authenticated and forever grounded her spiritual standing.

Humble, she guards her experiences.

Sharon continues to learn, mastering spiritual disciplines of the east and west as she fulfills her divine mission.

Living Life as A Sacred Practice: Discover Yourself as a Source of Creation encapsulates decades of learning that challenged her resolve, her character, her spiritual pedigree.

Now, Sharon offers her counsel and guidance to us.

Every word is judiciously used. Every sentence intuitively carved. Every stanza measured with deliberation.

Such is her wisdom.

And we are moved. We listen and reflect. Her words ring true.

"Humanity is entering the Age of Aquarius where harmony, peace and love will be the currency of exchange," she pens.

Know Thyself is the beginning of wisdom, the Aristotelian adage tells us. Sharon reinforces this principle. Love ourselves we are told. How else can we be of service to others?

Sharon takes our hand, guiding us through this awe-inspiring, cathartic affirmation:

"I am saying to my heart, I love you. I am your comforter and friend; I am sorry for any wrong that I have done; please forgive me and I thank you for allowing this problem to surface so that it can be eliminated." [Excerpt from Ho'oponopono]

She then expounds, "I must first recognize in me the need to heal myself, to heal my soul through speaking to my heart with these words.

These words reach the subconscious mind and transform your negative energies into pure love."[Excerpt from Ho'oponopono]

Living Life as a Sacred Practice is a literary monument that unravels life's deepest, overarching mysteries.

Life is a gift to be nurtured Sharon tells us; that our existence is profoundly meaningful, and that we are sparks of the living God.

Indeed, no greater personage than Jesus brought us this message in John 10:34. Centuries later, Sharon Oshun Parris-Chambers has dared to echo the same.

Glenville Ashby, PhD
Award-winning author and therapist
Member of Oxford University Philosophy Society (UK) and The International Society of Applied Psychoanalysis (France)

The Importance of Meditative Sacred Practice

Living Life as a Sacred Practice is the author's response to many years of trying to learn various methods of unifying mind, body, and spirit. She has captured the essence of life and greatness in this book with the inclusion of many practices to develop spiritual mastery.

The approach requires choosing a theme from the table of contents that resonates with the reader or on which the reader needs to work. Examples of suggested sections are: Abundance, Beauty, Breath Consciousness, Sacred Feminine, Healing, Inside Out, Life, Light, Sacred Feminine &Wellness. The process begins with reflecting on a Quotation, the Commentary, actively engage in the Sacred Meditative Practice, followed by reciting an Affirmation. This can be repeated throughout the day to reinforce the message.

You may choose a practice for twenty-one to thirty days to achieve spiritual transformation, or just use the suggested one that comes along with the quote for inspiration.

The commentaries are unique, thoughtful, and out of this world. It teaches the reader to be an original thinker and to look at life from the vantage point of a creator, not as an object of creation.

The author is a truth seeker, creator of transformational quotes and poetic prose, in which she has developed spiritual mastery over a span of twenty years. She shares these practices with readers seeking spiritual development.

She has expanded her focus on self-mastery with this new book, which asks the reader to come up higher to Divine Mind to find their purpose in life and to live that purpose.

A devotee of Dr Wayne Dyer, following his work during his life, she has transformed her life with the power of intention and practice. She now shares these practices with others.

The book is a tribute to Dr. Wayne Dyer one of her most influential mentors and to her husband and mentor, Theo Chambers.

The author is a non-denominational minister (BA) and has a BA in Psychology.

Just for a minute, lose yourself, get out of your conscious mind; then you can discover who you really are.
–Sharon Parris-Chambers

DIVINE CONSCIOUSNESS

I Embrace me and Love me is a prayer of Forgiveness.
–Sharon Parris-Chambers

"I embrace me as my authentic self; I look within

I no longer seek ego-gratification

I embrace me and love my reverent self

I am not in denial or fear my greatness

I will not run away from me, nor my brilliance

I am great beyond belief

I smile and relax in my being

I am no longer afraid of fear, failure or my shortcomings

I repeat these Healing Words of Ho'oponopono:

I love you, I am Sorry, Please Forgive me and Thank you

These special words heal our broken, tired hearts and lift our spirits.

SACRED PRACTICE:

Repeat as a Mantra for 5-10 mins and feel the power of this meditative affirmation. When used as a daily cleansing and healing ritual, it becomes a powerful tool for spiritual transformation. Ho'oponopono is an excellent complement for all forms of self-improvement, including meditation, yoga and life coaching, just to name a few.

Affirmation: Place your hand on your Heart and say:

"I love you, I am sorry, Please Forgive me and I thank you"

The meaning of Ho'oponopono ~ Hawaiian affirmation for forgiveness and healing, follows:

I am saying to my heart, I love you, I am your comforter and friend. I am sorry for any wrong that I have done; please forgive me and I thank you for allowing this problem to surface so that it can be eliminated.

I must first recognize in me the need to heal myself, to heal my soul through speaking to my heart with these words.

These words reach the subconscious mind and transform your negative energies into pure love. *"I love you, I am sorry, please forgive me and I thank you"*

When you use this practice and these words, you Clean, Delete and Cancel negative thoughts from the subconscious self and transform your negative energies into pure LOVE.

Love is the vibrational frequency that changes each person into Divine beings.

~~~~~~~~~~~~~~~

Personal Vignette

Throughout my life, as far back as my adolescence, I have been in search of my higher self. I travelled to the hills of St. Andrew, Mt. Charles, Mavis Bank, 17 miles outside of Kingston, Jamaica, to visit my grandparents. There in the hills alone, I had hoped to find God in the heavens.

I recited the psalms from the Christian Holy Scriptures, and sat in quiet contemplation. I enjoyed the fresh, clean air and warm sunshine. I did not know it then, but I grew in understanding, as nature took on new meaning. I was drawn to its nourishing tranquility.

My appreciation for nature was boundless; the clean rivers teeming with shrimp (Janga fresh water shrimp) and fish, the lush vegetation, the produce, the fruit trees, mangoes, grapefruits, peaches (yes we grew peaches in the cool verdant hills of Mt Charles). And there was something more.

I recall Grandpa Eustace cultivating the farm, raising the cattle and helping to transport produce to the market. Granny Estella nurtured the family, lived peacefully with our neighbours, and taught values, of which peace, love, honesty and compassion were foremost. Leaving Kingston to visit my grandparents in a rural Jamaica that was cradled in the valley of the awesome Blue Mountains over 7,000 feet high, brought me closer to my extended family - aunts, uncles and cousins. To experience nature while learning from one's elders forever shaped my life.

It built character and instilled an enduring sense of determination and responsibility to self and duty. More importantly, it sealed a bond with nature, an inviolable connection to Mother Earth, the feminine principle that lives in me... and every member of the global family.

This quest was my search for answers from the Goddess of my soul, my Divine self.

I AM my Conscious Awakening in the Now
–Sharon Parris-Chambers

This morning, I awoke like a lotus flower revealing its beauty to the world. Awaking to a new day, a New Year of great promise. Moving from a state of sleep to perceived reality. It can be likened to a rose opening its colorful and dainty petals to allow light. In this mindset, my inner and outer beauty become one. I step out living life from the inside out. Now, I speak from my own heart with the clearest of visions, unmoved by the fractured world that surrounds me. I call into creation what I seek; with every breath my intention, my creation is realized.

Seek by holding the intention with every breath you take.

Now, focus your intention and BECOME. Open your heart to receive, to BECOME, TO MATERIALIZE all that you deserve. The magnanimity of the Universe will astound you. This practice is to learn to trust with your whole soul. Open your arms high above your head to receive the abundance that awaits you. The Universe is unfailing, ever returning what is owed to us.

Throughout my life, I have sought direction. I have tried repeatedly to picture my ideal life. What seemed like an exercise in futility blossomed into an exercise demanding intention, focus and deliberation.

I began to create an image of my spiritual partner. The process was long, but patient I was. And expectedly, my visualization bore fruit. The Universe responded bestowing much more than anticipated. A life of comfort with a partner of my dreams is a gift, the perfect gift from the Giver of all things.

Living life as an Intuitive Presence, seeking to harm no one or anything, generates karmic rewards that manifest in so many ways.

Be patient. Time is an illusion. Stay focused and allow God to do the rest.

Sacred Practice: Sit in quiet reflection observing your breath for 15 mins. Perform the asanas in the Sun Salutation. Return to 15 minutes of reflection. Write your experiences in your journal.

Affirmation: *I am open and receptive to the Divine universe*

Note: **Write your Affirmations and reflections in your journal daily. At the end of the week, return to the beginning of each week to reflect and to learn about your remarkable self.**

I AM MY I AM PRESENCE

I AM my I AM presence and I acknowledge this awareness as Divine presence in me right now.

Humanity is entering the Age of Aquarius where harmony, peace and love will be the currency of exchange.

I give thanks to my lineage through which I entered the planet. We can invoke the light of God for everyone on earth simultaneously. Not just one person, but to *seven and a half billion* people on the planet.

Accepting the changes unfolding before me. I allow my I AM presence to take charge of transforming my mind and body to enter this celestial period on earth.

Say: "*I invoke the light of God on behalf of myself, my loved ones and all humanity.*"

Meditative Practice: Sit in quiet reflection. Focus on your breath. For 15 -30 minutes, inhale, exhale and relax as you repeat the mantra: "*I invoke the light of God on behalf of myself, my loved ones and all humanity.*"

Your thoughts can become aimless and restless when you sit in meditation. Use the mantra above to guide your thoughts. Smile and be positive. Breathe deeply, inhale and exhale until you are in a state of deep relaxation. If you are tense, breathe into that tense area. Let your breath soothe away trepidation and worry. Do not wrestle with your thoughts. Release them.

Your breath is your guide during these explorations. Meditation is no mystery. It really is a state of mind, not an activity. Meditation is a state that is entered. Adept, we can access the deeper layers of the mind, the spiritual realm – our original home. Your journey home will become easier, more accessible. This home is the reservoir of all good, all healing, all creativity. Here, there is no negativity, no evil. The home we know is harmonious, peaceful. It is from this place that humanity is redeemed.

Affirmation: *I AM My I AM presence.*

Your Presence is a Present to humanity
–Sharon Parris-Chambers

Today you acknowledge your presence as a present to humanity. Your presence is not an accident. Some may believe so and some may not. However, in *patois* (Jamaican language), We say "who fi de yah, de yah". Your divinity before your physical manifestation determined your incarnation on earth and your purpose. When you manifested in physical form, you forgot your Divine nature. That is why truth seekers stress knowing your purpose. When you remember your purpose and focus on it, you begin to reconnect to your Divine Self and your soul's journey.

Excessive Pride, Fame, Materialism and Greed are not Divine attributes and will lead you down a path far from realizing your true potential. When your intention is set on discovering your true potential and capacity for greatness, you recognize that your presence is a present, A GIFT to humanity.

Today, make the shift from earthbound to Divine. Live life from the inside out. Actively choose meditation to find answers to life's troubles. Depression, anger, and self-medication are not viable answers. Through daily reflection you begin to understand the forces that are hindering your God-given abilities.

Sacred Practice: Sit in a quiet place, clear your mind of distractions. Begin to breathe, taking long inhalations and then long exhalations. When you begin to feel relaxed, create in your mind's eye a picture of happiness, joy and laughter. Recall moments in time that took your breath away. Saturate your mind with these pleasant images. Just be in this moment.

Ego distractions always appear when you sit for meditation. Just be in this moment. Create your intentions for the day, ask your questions, such as: "What is my purpose in life?" "What am I to do and how am I to do it?" Continue to sit in meditation and the answers will come, if not then, later. But they will.

Write down the thoughts and answers to your questions. Do this every day and night to develop the pattern of listening to your Higher Self, your Divine Self.

Affirmation: *My presence is a Divine Gift.*

True Beauty

See the beauty in all beings and
you see the beauty in you.
–Sharon Parris-Chambers

Sharon Parris-Chambers
Selfie

When you practice seeing the beauty in the human experience and in all beings, you also see the beauty in yourself.

You learn to value, to love and honor you. This is sacred practice, remember Christ Jesus, the anointed one, asked us in the Holy Bible scriptures to love our neighbor as our self. This is a Sacred practice – to love the Divinity within us. This is a solemn duty that could change the world. If we love our neighbors as we love ourselves, honor and respect them, we can begin to be the change we wish to see in the world. This is the African Ubuntu principle at work. *"I am because we are."*

Sacred Practice:
Practice looking in the mirror daily. Immerse your senses in your mirror image before you and say: "I love you." You will begin to heal the child within with these words.

Another effective practice is looking into the heart of a freshly cut Rose. Find a quiet place in nature or in the quiet of your room. Begin to stare at the center of the Rose, its heart. A Rose is much like life: you will encounter obstacles – thorns along the way, but with faith and belief you will experience the essence of the flower, the very divinity of your being.

Keep staring at the rose. Notice its color, texture and design. Savor its fragrances and think only about this thing of beauty in front of you. At first, other thoughts will enter your mind, gently say, "I will deal with this later." Simply return your attention to the object of your focus. Soon your mind will grow strong and disciplined.

Excerpt - "The Heart of the Rose" from *The Monk who sold his Ferrari.* (Sharma, 2007)

When you practice seeing the beauty in you and humanity, you will begin to develop a spiritual consciousness and a disciplined mind that will lead to the desires of your heart. Live your passion and dreams. Practice this exercise regularly and manifest your destiny.

Affirmation: *I see the beauty in me and humanity.*

Spiritual Beauty

Beauty is not skin deep, it is soul
deep, intuitive and spiritual.
–Sharon Parris-Chambers

Be a true beauty queen in and out of the boardroom. It is an attitude, a discipline and a way of life. A woman who has been properly groomed for success should first learn about the social graces, etiquette, beauty care. *She does not have to be a model or a beauty queen, just act like one.* That means, she moves with grace, style, diplomacy and knows the social etiquette of being in public. Therefore, her personal grooming, speech and decorum must be informed by proper training, which begins around seven years of age, during the time she is developing concrete thinking, pre-puberty. (Piaget).

For more information on beauty etiquette, send email to: parrischambers@gmail.com

Sacred Practice:
Love the person that you see in the mirror every day. On awakening, go to the mirror. Look at your reflection. Say to the bare face person staring at you, I LOVE YOU, MWAH (Kiss your reflection.) When you can do this without criticism. You are ready to face the world!

Affirmation: *I AM Beauty personified.*

Live Life as a Creator not a Piece of Creation
–Sharon Parris-Chambers

You are a Divine being, I am a Divine being, born as a spark of creation. How can you or I be any less? You are a microcosm of the Divine universe. Why downgrade and weaken your capacity? You are a source of creation with potentiality to achieve great things. Say, *"I open myself to the greatness that I AM as a Source of Creation. I am a Creator, ideas flow through me easily and readily like the river flows to the sea. I write my truths, I speak my word sounds into creation. My thoughts and words become reality, I am a Creator of great ideas and things."*

As the inner muse speaks to you, you become aware of your past cellular memory: "I remember my connection to my Ankhsestors (Ancestors) who were gods & goddesses, the foundation of civilization, creators of great Kingdoms, pyramids, founders of libraries, creators of the sciences, scribes, first doctors, sculptors/artists, poets, navigators, space time travelers, etc. If this were not true, how could they have been transplanted to new worlds, and become the harbingers of knowledge to re-create pyramids, step-pyramids, create the New World of the Americas, and help to industrialize Europe?"

If you doubt this, then you relegate yourself to an object of creation, you give away your potentiality and develop poverty consciousness where things just happen to you. You don't make things happen. Let us deal with this shift right now, moving from poverty consciousness to enlightenment (Satori).

Sacred Practice: Breathe deeply, exhale and relax. Enter meditation. Your only focus is: "I am the Source of Creation not a piece of creation. I command my mind, body and spirit to raise my conscious awareness of who I am. I reach out to my Ankhsestors and connect with each one…" Call their names. After calling their names, continue to breathe deeply and focus on the Mantra. Write down all thoughts and ideas that arise.

Ritual Practice: Offering to Ankhsestors (Ancestors-gods). This is an additional step for those who perform Rituals. Go to the ocean or water source. Open with prayer, then make an offering to goddess Oshun (mother of sweet waters or fresh water) or in her form as mother of salt water, goddess Yemanja). Take honey (sweetness), ground coffee (alertness) beans & rice (abundance), milk (generativity), salt (protection) offer to goddess Oshun/Yemanja, ask for what you want, give thanks and close with prayer.

After making ritual offerings to the goddesses/orishas, you may choose to make an offering to the Ankhsestors. Do so now and give thanks and close the session.

Affirmation: *I AM a Creator not a piece of creation.*

*Tune in to Divine Spirit, an ever-
ready and ever-present source.*
–Sharon Parris-Chambers

There is no barrier to Divine Love and Light. You can access these frequencies right now. Open your heart and Enter.

Remove the barriers of hate, fear, protectionism, anger, anxiety and racial divisions. Accept each human being as your friend, brother and sister. We belong to the human family, one race. We are homo sapiens. However, when the third eye is open, these divisions melt away; only a oneness remains. The key is to access awareness of who you really are, your power and purpose. This should take precedence over material wealth. All things are added when we first seek the Kingdom of knowledge and become aware of the Divine Self. Take a moment to process this admonition from the Holy Bible Scriptures (Matthew 6:33): "But seek first the kingdom of God and his righteousness, and all these things will be added to you." (English Standard Version)

Where is the kingdom? Prevailing thought leaders in the metaphysical science identify the Kingdom as a transcendental, pure state of mind. The inner core of the human being has never been fully explored. There is no complexity, just fear of the unknown. This fear is akin to exploration of the arctic space and the depths of the ocean.

Now, there is a sustained effort to explore outer regions of space. This same push is happening in our inner core, the spiritual self. Open your heart and consciousness to what you really are: of mind, body and spirit.

Practice accessing the 'Kingdom' daily. Take time morning and evening to unwind. It is critical to do this during these times of fear, discord, racism, bigotry and wars. These expressions do not come from Gaia - Earth Mother - but from fear-based energy systems. There is great need to rebalance earth to experience the peace and harmony of this New Age of Aquarius.

The old paradigms are falling away. Look – open your eyes. Look at the responses of people the world over to racial profiling and racial discrimination. In the USA, citizens are fighting for protection of freedom of speech and worship. They are fighting to protect the First and Second Amendments. There is a groundswell of social and political consciousness that is challenging the Old Order. It is a global movement, like no other.

The Shift, a movie conceived by Dr Wayne Dyer, is taking place now. We must open our Third Eye. We are called to fulfill our divine responsibilities and advance the agenda of Spirit. All creation must come into harmony with Universal Law for earth to be realigned and recalibrated from the polarizing forces of hate, fear, war and crime. We must work together to salvage earth. We owe it to ourselves and progeny. We owe it to Gaia, Earth Mother, our Mother.

Sacred Practice: Divine Healing Breaths.
Sit in meditation daily for 15 to 30 minutes. Inhale and exhale, relax. Choose a short phrase or mantra (*"I am a clear channel for Divine good"*) to direct your thoughts.

Keeping the breath even:

1) Breathe in and hold for count of 12
2) Exhale for count of 12
3) Breathe in and hold for count of 12
4) Exhale for count of 12

Repeat this cycle 10 times. Relax at the end of all ten (10) cycles.

Journal your experiences.

Affirmations:
I am a Potent Powerhouse of Potentiality; I can access Divine Spirit with each breath.

Choose to Stop suffering now by shifting your
Memory and Imagination to a more positive space.
–Sharon Parris-Chambers

Today marks the first day of the rest of your life. Live your life, exert your positive intentions or let Life Live You and exert its unknown intentions upon you.

Stop suffering by removing lack and limitation from your mind and imagination. You are what you think! Vision yourself the way you want to be. Shift - Focus and re-Connect to a new Conscious and Visual image of yourself. Make a conscious decision to stop suffering NOW!

Leave yesterday in the dustbin of eternity. Suffering is NOT a way of life. Cancel, Cancel and Cancel all negative thoughts and Images. Transforming the personality takes time. So be patient. Begin to consciously Cancel negative thoughts, saying the words: Cancel, Cancel, Cancel. With practice, clearing, canceling negative and repressed thoughts in the subconscious, eventually you will become more positive, and harmonious.

There are many ways to clear and cancel negative thoughts, here are a few: Neurolinguistic Programming (NLP), Emotional Freedom Technique (EFT) and Ho'oponopono, a Hawaiian practice of reconciliation and forgiveness using the words: "I love you, I am sorry, please forgive me, and thank you." These words used repeatedly brings the individual back to Love. According to Dr. Ihaleakala Hew Len, author of Zero Limits, we must "constantly clean, clean, clean. You have to clean on anything and everything, as you have no idea what is a memory and what is inspiration."

Choose today to Live your life or Let Life Live you!

Sacred Practice: Stand in front of the mirror and speak to your mirror image. Cross your hands over your heart and gaze into your eyes. Say: "I love me and I honor me." "I will never allow anyone to hurt or abuse me." "I will never give up on me." "I love my life and enjoy being alive."

Then turn it around as if you are the Coach speaking and say: "I love you and I honor you." "I will never allow anyone to hurt or abuse you." I will never give up on you." Love the life you live and enjoy yourself."

Smile and visualize the feeling of being loved by your parents, friends and family. Enjoy these vibrations. Repeat as often as necessary.

Affirmation: *I choose to Live Life to the Fullest!*

I AM a Divine Being transmitting Divine Love.
—Sharon Parris-Chambers

As you evolve spiritually you will understand the inner meaning of the following: There is no other being like me in the universe. I AM love and love's Divine expression.

The life force moves through me, a microcosm of the universe, vibrating and expressing its desires to interpret and reinterpret itself. I AM a channel of Love and Light.

I relax in awareness that the universe moves me, and I am one with the Divine universe. I free my mind from day to day worries and concerns so that, effortlessly, the universe expresses through me.

Sacred Practice: Practice daily the Law of Least Effort by visualizing what you want to enter into your life.

I first encountered The Law of Least Effort during my study of Deepak Chopra's book: *"The Seven Laws of Spiritual Success"* and I share it with you now:

A. *I will practice Acceptance. Today I will accept people, situations, circumstances, and events as they occur. I will know that this moment is as it should be, because the whole universe is as it should be. I will not struggle against the whole universe by struggling against this moment. My acceptance is total and complete. I accept things as they are this moment, not as I wish they were.*

B. *Having accepted things as they are, I will take Responsibility for my situation and for all those events I see as problems. I know that taking responsibility means not blaming anyone or anything for my situation (and this includes myself). I also know that every problem is an opportunity in disguise, and this alertness to opportunities allows me to take this moment and transform it into a greater benefit.*

C. *Today my awareness will remain established in Defenselessness. I will relinquish the need to defend my point of view, and I will feel no need to persuade others to accept my point of view. I will remain open to all points of view and not be rigidly attached to any one of them. (https://chopra.com)*

I go into a quiet zone and visualize what I wish to manifest. Doing this regularly creates a shift from the *unmanifest* (unconscious) to *manifest*(conscious) state. Practice the Law of Least Effort often, through its application you will transform into your Divine Self.

Affirmation: I am a microcosm of the universe.

*Live Life as though you were given a second
chance to manifest your destiny.*
–Sharon Parris-Chambers

Have you ever been face to face with a life or death situation? Did you feel as though you had a Second Chance at life?

How did you respond? Do you have support systems that you can rely on or are you going it alone? These are important questions to contemplate during your quiet reflection times that you set aside. **Imagine the life you want to live and then actively live it one moment at a time.**

Do not waste any time living in the past. Every moment and every thought represent your life. Live life one moment at a time. It appears that multi-tasking is the way of the world. However, when you live from inside out, you may want to make some adjustments. Slow down, breathe and learn to find your own productive pace.

Live in the Now. Take time to reflect on where your life is taking you or where you are going in life. When you take time to reflect on your life you will be deliberate and purposeful in your actions.

Life offers no guarantees. It requires that you live in accordance with universal laws that govern your body temple and Mother Earth (Gaia or the environment). You live 24/7 in your body. So, it is important to take care of your body. Get your annual medical checks. Eat raw, organic foods; and drink clean, spring water as often as possible. Detox the body system regularly, use enemas to remove mucus and waste.

It is also important to exercise regularly several times a week to maintain good health.

Commit to living a conscious and holistic lifestyle today!

Sacred Practice: Choose a practice from the Appendix.

Affirmation: *I Live in the present moment of Eternity.*

When you see with your heart, you relieve the eyes
of the lie of illusion and see with true clarity.
–Sharon Parris-Chambers

Your eyes reflect images that are transmitted by your thoughts. Change your thoughts and you change your vision. Cognitive and social psychologists say we have a sensory filter or 'schemata'. Everything passes through that filter. Every human being has the same filter mechanism. Sometimes we choose to see things with 'rose colored glasses' and at other times, we just want the truth. Truth seekers want to really see, to break through the illusion and see with clarity. That's when one turns to seeing with the heart, which never lies, it knows the soul's journey and is the spirit guide.

Sacred Practice: Sit in a quiet place. Take some deep breaths, relax. Find the center of your being. Resonate in this awareness as a conscious sentient being. Continue taking deep breaths. *Explore the thoughts of who is the "Secret Person of the Heart?" or "Who Am I as Consciousness or the Observer?"* Write your thoughts in your journal.

Think of yourself as you truly are, as Consciousness, Energy and Vibration. The Force that is breathing you. Remove the thoughts *of me, myself, mother, brother, sister, husband or wife* right now. You are *Consciousness*. Moving and flowing in creation. You can take any form. You are boundless and you create effortlessly through your thoughts and imagination. You can always come to this place to restore, re-create, rejuvenate, revivify and resurrect your spirit. There is no lack here, the vibration of love and light abounds. Hold this conscious intention now and throughout the day. Return here any time you need inspiration and rejuvenation.

Affirmation: *I see without illusions.*

Experience Divine enlightenment right now!
–Sharon Parris-Chambers

You can have the Christ mind, Buddha mind or mind of Krishna right now. Let go of fear and walk in Divine light. Commitment to truth and obedience to Spirit will lead you to enlightenment.

Awake from your slumber and transcend to a new level of awareness. Experience Divine light and love when you listen to the still small voice within guiding you to your ultimate good. Go ahead, listen with an open heart and you will hear it. It is a vibration; a conscious lifestyle. Just open your heart and trust Divine spirit. You will awaken to a whole new world. The awakening experience is called Satori. In fact, you can spend your whole life seeking Satori, and never really 'find' it. 'Why' do you ask? Because Satori is experienced during each moment of awareness.

Sacred Practice: Contemplate a Koan of your choice.

Note: Koans are an ancient tradition of stories, phrases, poems or statements that were identified, though the years, for their transformational ability. Sometimes a koan is a recounting of the circumstances that lead to the awakening of a particular student. Sometimes they shock. Sometimes they confuse, but always, the koan interacts with something deeper than the mind.

A koan may appear non-nonsensical, but a koan is not a riddle or a puzzle. It cannot be solved by understanding it. Only when it opens you up to something new about your true nature, when something in you shifts in response, will you become intimate with the koan.

Sit in Zazen while assuming the lotus posture. Choose a koan. Contemplate.

☐ When the many are reduced to one, to what is the one reduced?
☐ When you can do nothing, what can you do?
☐ What is your original face before you were born?
☐ Create one of your own.
(The Buddhaful Tao, 2012)

Write your answers in your journal. All answers are relevant. It is the experience that matters most.

Affirmation: I live in the Chi of life and walk in Divine light.

Are You Open to Divine Flow of Consciousness?
—Sharon Parris-Chambers

You are entitled to your private moments with Divine Spirit. Many years ago, while attending the Whole Life Expo in Atlanta, GA, 1998, I met Neale Donald Walsch, the author of the book series, **Conversations with God**. What a privil*ege to have conversations with God; don't we all have these conversations? He said I can also have these experiences. He mentioned his openness to Divine source as key to his mystical experiences and the source of his authorship.*

Are you open to God's expressions in your life? Can you feel and interpret divine vibration? It is one of peace and love. Listen. Be obedient and allow it to speak to you. As you continue to allow the Divine in your life, you will experience a conscious shift in your being. You will develop the desire to continue to express goodness in your own way, as did Neale Donald Walsch who asked many pertinent questions in his work. He shared his experiences with the world.

Let's explore some of these questions: What is your truth? With whom are you sharing it? What is your life's purpose? Is God speaking in and through you or, are you allowing the world to edit your Divine flow. Is the world taking you for a puppet, turning you and twisting you around? Or, are you standing on solid ground, open to the flow of Divine consciousness? Are you allowing Divine Spirit to animate you with every breath and to manifest in your life?

It is time to come back to Love as our Constant Source of Divine Good. Every day is a glorious day as you learn to receive and give this vibration of Love to those around you. Most important is your ability to love yourself unconditionally.

Sacred Practice:
Sit in quiet meditation or reflection, allowing no thought interference for 15-30 minutes. Remain calm and quiet, open to the sensory and vibratory sensations of your body.

Bask in quietude. Write your experience in your journal.

Affirmation:
I Allow Thoughts of Goodness, Beauty, and Peace to fill my Mind…and My Life is Filled with Goodness, Beauty, and Peace.
(Heraldess Adama Alaji ~ www.Adamaspeaks.com)

> *When you obstruct the flow of Divine Law of the*
> *Universe, you will feel its effect in mind, body and spirit.*
> —*Sharon Parris-Chambers*

Nothing can stop your flow of Divine good or energy but you. Therefore, find a way under, over or around any obstacle that would upset your Divine energy, peace and balance. You are the master of your destiny. You are the one you have been waiting for. You have Greatness within. Rise to the occasion and accept your Greatness. Let nothing obstruct your flow of Divine good, Divine Intelligence, Divine Greatness.

Now, if you DO allow obstructions to your Divine flow, then you will feel Dis-ease in your mind, body and spirit. The universal Law is what it is, immutable. Find a way to obey the Universal law and enjoy the blessings of peace, love and happiness all the days of your life.

Sacred Practice: Find time today to breathe deeply, relax and affirm your Divine Good. For example: *I am in union with Divine Spirit.* Take a minimum of 5-15 minutes and relax into your breath. Breathe in – Hold for count of 12, Breathe out -for Count of 12. Breathe in-Hold for a count of 12. Exhale for count of 12 and Repeat for 10 cycles. Relax and resume normal deep breathing.

You will receive benefits in mind, body and spirit as you continue to sit in meditation. Allow your breath to breathe you, becoming relaxed, you experience the union of mind, body and spirit.

Affirmation: *I am in union with Divine Spirit.*

SACRED FEMININE

Then creation recognized its Creator in
its own forms and appearances.
For in the beginning, when God said, "Let it be!"
and it came to pass, the means and the
Matrix of creation was Love,
because all creation was formed through
Her as in the twinkling of an eye.
- Sapientia St. Hildegard von Bingen

The Matrix Of Creation

"The feminine is the matrix of creation. This truth is something profound and elemental, and every woman knows it in the cells of her body, in her instinctual depths. Out of the substance of her very being life comes forth. She can conceive and give birth, participate in the greatest mystery of bringing a soul into life. And yet we have forgotten, or been denied, the depths of this mystery, of how the divine light of the soul creates a body in the womb of a woman, and how the mother shares in this wonder, giving her own blood, her own body, to what will be born. Our culture's focus on a disembodied, transcendent God has left women bereft, denying them the sacredness of this simple mystery of divine love.

What we do not realize is that this patriarchal denial affects not only every woman, but also life itself. When we deny the divine mystery of the feminine we also deny something fundamental to life. We separate life from its sacred core, from the matrix that nourishes all of creation. We cut our world off from the source that alone can heal, nourish and transform it. The same sacred source that gave birth to each of us is needed to give meaning to our life, to nourish it with what is real, and to reveal to us the mystery, the divine purpose to being alive."

Because humanity has a central function in the whole of creation, what we deny to ourself we deny to all of life. In denying the feminine her sacred power and purpose we have impoverished life in ways we do not understand. We have denied life its sacred source of meaning and divine purpose, which was understood by the ancient priestesses. We may think that their fertility rites and other ceremonies belonged only to the need for procreation or a successful harvest. In our contemporary culture we cannot understand how a deeper mystery was enacted, one that consciously connected life to its source in the inner worlds, a source that held the wholeness of life as an embodiment of the divine, allowing the wonder of the divine to be present in every moment.

Source: (Vaughn-Lee, 2007)

The Ascension Of The Sacred Feminine

The Divine Feminine as the Matrix of Creation
—Sharon Parris-Chambers

I am the Sacred Feminine that was silenced by those who wanted to ascend my throne, to brush me aside into obscurity in the ash heaps of eternity. However, like Isis & Osiris, I gathered my consciousness, other parts and reconnected to my greatness.

I am the Sacred Feminine, the Mother of Creation, the Mother Goddess, I am that I AM, Goddess Eternal. I and my sister Gaia, Mother Earth, are one.

We have ascended to the Throne to love, forgive, honor, respect and teach our mystical truth as the Sage Within, never to be silenced in this generation. We will reveal the feminine nature in males and females awakening the Yin and Yang in every being and their connection to the universe.

We will use nature's electromagnetic force, the energetic field, to reconnect to humanity. We are ready to express our magical arts to speak, think and move at the speed of light, that's right, my sisters! We are entering Mach time, vibrating at the speed of light and love. We are Love, we are Peace; we are the Womb of Creation.

Repeat after me, "I AM Love, I AM Peace, I AM the Womb of Creation, I AM, I AM, I AM, I AM."

Connecting with your Goddess Self. Ascend your Divine throne. Assume your rightful place. Never will you be looked down on, stamped on, thrown out of churches, bibles, sacred texts, dishonored, placed behind men, hidden from yourself and other female Goddesses. Those who seek and have sought to hide you are being removed, uprooted and silenced.

Yes, Earth Mother is hurtling through space faster than ever in her history to arrive at this moment when earth's axis is tilted back to the time when the Sacred Feminine is honored, worshipped and elevated.

We the womb, the incubator, the tree of life cannot be replaced. Cut the umbilical cord, yes you are on your own, but Mother Earth still looks after you. Connect with her, ground yourself in her, honor and love her as you love yourself. You will become balanced, whole and spiritually grounded.

You arrive at this sacred space when you can say: "I AM a reflection of Mother Earth, I AM the Sacred Feminine, I AM a goddess born into creation each moment, ever manifesting in the now. And so it is."

VALUES TO LIVE BY

Values to Live By: Ma'at

When we reflect on values to live by, the forty-two laws of Ma'at (also known as Mayet) comes to mind. Ma'at, the ancient Egyptian goddess of truth, justice, morality, and balance first appeared during the period known as the Old Kingdom (c. 2613 - 2181 BCE) or earlier.

Ma'at is characterized as a winged goddess in hieroglyphics and in literature. She is depicted in profile, which is the artistic cannon of the time, wearing her trademarked ostrich feather on her head. Sometimes, just as a white ostrich feather glyph, representing truth.

These principles of life guided the Egyptian (Kemetic) civilization and can also guide our modern civilization today. In fact, the Judeo-Christian Ten Commandments takes its reference from the Laws of Ma'at.

MA'AT – Principles of Life: Truth, Justice, Morality, Law, Balance, Harmony & Order.

Transgressions Against Mankind

1. I have not committed murder, neither have I bid any man to slay on my behalf;

2. I have not committed rape, neither have I forced any woman to commit fornication;

3. I have not avenged myself, nor have I burned with rage;

4. I have not caused terror, nor have I worked affliction;

5. I have caused none to feel pain, nor have I worked grief;

6. I have done neither harm nor ill, nor have I caused misery;

7. I have done no hurt to man, nor have I wrought harm to beasts;

8. I have made none to weep;

9. I have had no knowledge of evil, neither have I acted wickedly, nor have I wronged the people;

10. I have not stolen, neither have I taken that which does not belong to me, nor that which belongs to another, nor have I taken from the orchards, nor snatched the milk from the mouth of the babe;

11. I have not defrauded, neither have I added to the weight of the balance, nor have I made light the weight in the scales;

12. I have not laid waste the plowed land, nor trampled down the fields;

13. I have not driven the cattle from their pastures, nor have I deprived any of that which was rightfully theirs;

14. I have accused no man falsely, nor have I supported any false accusation;

15. I have spoken no lies, neither have I spoken falsely to the hurt of another;

16. I have never uttered fiery words, nor have I stirred up strife;

17. I have not acted guilefully, neither have I dealt deceitfully, nor spoken to deceive or to hurt another;

18. I have not spoken scornfully, nor have I set my lips in motion against any man;

19. I have not been an eavesdropper;

20. I have not stopped my ears against the words of Right and Truth;

21. I have not judged hastily, nor have I judged harshly;

22. I have committed no crime in the place of Right and Truth;

23. I have caused no wrong to be done to the servant by his master;

24. I have not been angry without cause;

25. I have not turned back water at its springtide, nor stemmed the flow of running water;

26. I have not broken the channel of a running water;

27. I have never fouled the water, nor have I polluted the land;

Transgressions Against the Gods 28-37 have been omitted due to space constraints.

Personal Transgressions

28. I have not acted guilefully, nor have I acted in insolence;

29. I have not been overly proud, nor have I behaved myself with arrogance;

30. I have never magnified my condition beyond what was fitting;

31. Each day have I labored more than was required of me;

32. My name has not come forth to the boat of the Prince.

If we cannot keep our minds peaceful, how can the world be peaceful? The world outside is a reflection of the human mind.
-By Sadhguru

Values Of Ma'at

Peace

In a world full of change and uncertainty, do not be afraid, retreat to your Temple of Inner Peace for guidance, strength and vision.
–Sharon Parris-Chambers

The world's overt and subtle pressures derail us from the path of enlightenment. Confused, we seek material things for validation, all the while struggling to stay afloat.

Stop! Guard against destructive influences. Take charge of your Temple.

Let us focus on what is best for developing the mind, body and spirit. If my mind is at peace I am unmoved by the battering noise. I am still, unmoved by the vacuous chatter. I am in charge. My choices are mine – deliberate and balanced. How could I go wrong?

Sacred Practice: Retreat to your Temple of Inner Peace, go inward to your inner sanctuary. Focus on your breath; use breathing exercises to move the breath and allow these words to transport you to higher consciousness: "There is quiet there, an ocean of peace and tranquility permeates your consciousness. You are one with it. There is no separation. You escape your troubles in body and mind. You are pure energy and vibration. You think thoughts and they manifest in physical form. You emanate light; You are transformed into your subtle body. You are light, your original source.

Imagine this is your coach speaking; Repeat after me: *"I no longer blame others or myself for my behavior. I do not choose to blame as an escape or solution to my troubles, I retreat to my Temple of Inner Peace, my inner sanctuary, to find the answers. I face temporary situations head on and deal with the issues. This way, the demons that I make up in my mind are dissolved by tackling the real issues."*

Write your experiences in your journal.

Affirmation: *I live from my Temple of Inner Peace.*

I AM Peace Flowing unbounded in the universe.
–Sharon Parris-Chambers

Recognizing your essence as energy and vibration, you become aware of yourself as a wave, amid an ocean of peace.

You allow nothing to affect your energetic flow. Day by day you live as a sentient being of conscious awareness and love. Harbingers of doom do not disturb you. Deaths, wars and crime do not alter your peace. You remain at equilibrium.

Disturb your thought patterns and you begin to adversely affect the world. Don't project into the world the chaos and evil it has fed your mind.

Mental poisoning is a reality, a truth of which truth seekers are aware.

Taking time for meditative practice daily to empty the mind of fear, anxiety, hatred and discord will lead you closer to Divine consciousness, peace and love.

Moving from an 'earth-bound' consciousness to 'Divine' consciousness is the Shift that needs to take place now. Once you have reached this point of awareness, the task is to live from the subtle regions of consciousness and not from the dictates of the restless mind.

Sacred Practice: Affirm your Divine good with these words: "I am a Being of Peace and Love, I reflect that which I AM, not the rubbish from the world view of who I am. I AM a Divine being, a point of light and reflection of the Divine Universe."

Peace Mantra: *I AM Peace Flowing unbounded in the universe.*

(Repeat as often as needed.)

Peace is more than an absence of War, it is the innate state of a conscious Human Being.
–Sharon Parris-Chambers

We all long for peace in the world. Everyday there are images on the TV screen that impress on the screen of our minds that this is a dangerous world. Images of crime, death and dying, war, report of wars and weapons stockpiling on the nightly news.

Do not allow the excesses shared by the media daily to shake your composure. Allow what we know deep in the recesses of our soul to surface. There is an innate peace that pacifies the soul.

What if millions of people begin to do this? Do you believe we could positively impact the world with a different story?

There is a likelihood that we could begin to hear, feel, see images of beauty, kindness and experience more peaceful interactions as human beings, when we begin to live from our heart center and not from a fearful mind. This would erase the negative mental images. How much longer will we continue to absorb this negativity before we say, "No More!" Then, reach for the remote control and turn off the TV.

The words of Thomas Paine, published in the *American Crisis*, "these are the times that try men's souls," ring true today as it did back in 1776. However, if we stop and take a survey right now of where you live. You would find that in your inner core, your Temple, is your place to retreat from the world's man-made crises.

Take some time now to retreat to your Inner Temple, where there is quietude. There you will find your natural mindscape to paint pictures on the canvas of your mind, refreshing waters to cool your body and your thirst. Flora and fauna of the most exotic types. The soulscape is an untouched reservoir of primeval images, sounds and impressions tapped only in our dreams. There is no fear here, only the deep, deep peace that resounds, lulls and pacifies the soul. Retreat to your soulscape and find the hidden you.

Sacred Practice: Take the next 30 minutes to relax your body by taking some deep breaths. Go deep within. Follow your breath. Take strong even breaths, relax after each one. Welcome the godhead or goddess of your being and say you are ready to explore the spiritual you. Allow your inner vision to take over your physical faculties and explore the hidden you. Ask questions and listen for the answers which will arise in you as a SENSATION, feeling, voice, image or impression. Make a point to write in your journal when you return from your adventure.

Affirmation: *My peace flows within me like the river to the sea.*

Humility

Meet your Humility Halfway; Dare to be different.
–Sharon Parris-Chambers

Tune inward to your reverent power. Find your passion. It will take you to great heights.

On your journey, you will be challenged with lessons on humility. With spiritual practice you will learn humility, the key to entering the kingdom.

Is humility meekness? Humility is a value that comes from a deep place inside the human being. It drives one toward respect, kindness, forgiveness and love for humanity. It is an intrinsic part of a sentient experience.

The source of creation is within you. Therefore, rise to your greatness with humility at your core. Dare to be different! Believe in yourself and your reverent power to manifest your destiny one day at a time.

Sacred practice: Choose a meditative practice from the Appendix.

Affirmation: *Greatness lives in me.*

One Love

Unify the World Around One Love
—Sharon Parris-Chambers

One Love Call To Action & Pledge

When the Great Tempter, the enemy, masquerades as your friend and sends lightning rods of hatred and bigotry your way, gracefully and powerfully just deflect them with the wave of your hand. Your intention is to Send Love and Light to fight your Battles.

Let the God or Goddess of your being answer with Love, the most powerful vibration in the universe. Love and Light are twinned. The more Love you emote, the more Light you reflect.

Ancestors near and far, guide our transition from this dichotomous world of Love and Hate, Black and White, War and Peace to one of Harmony, Peace and Pure Love. LOVE IS LIGHT, LIGHT IS LOVE and GOD IS LOVE.

Are you willing to go through the fire that purges your internal demons so that you may be transformed into a being of love and light? Do you appreciate life every day and give thanks with every breath? Write your gratitude notes and your answers to these questions in your journal.

Sacred Practice: Unify the World Around One Love

Sit in meditation, begin to focus on your breath. Relax fully. Begin to visualize the earth as a small ball in your open hands. Send blessings of love and light to the earth. Reach deep within to access your Divine love and send it from your I AM Presence to the I AM presence of each person on earth through the ball. Focus your intention on the small ball in your hand, which is a symbol of earth. Continue for 15 minutes or more read or recite an inspirational Psalm, Poetry or Mantra of your choice to close your meditative practice.

You may do this exercise any time you wish to share love and light with your family, friends or humanity.

Affirmation: *I AM Love and Light*

Obedience

When ego has retreated; obedience to truth emerges.
—Sharon Parris-Chambers

Gandhi once said: *"The Voice for truth speaks to every person on the planet, every single day. That voice is as loud as our willingness to listen."*

If the voice for truth speaks to every single person on the planet daily, are you turned in to it? Know the voice for truth. Move toward it in your life. Turn your attention and your senses Up so that you can become obedient to truth speaking to you right now.

The Voice is sometimes characterized as "still and small". Whatever it is, whether fortissimo (loud) or pianissimo (soft) you need to learn synchronicity. Learn to dance with the music of the universe.

It is obedience that leads us to our ultimate good. It leads you by the hand on your path to your Divine appointment. Before you can really trust others, trust the god or goddess within. Then, you learn to submit to the will of your Divinity.

Sacred Practice: Mindfulness Meditation.

Mindfulness meditation also known as Vipassana and insight meditation, requires focus on mindfulness practice. It is awareness of the object of meditation, the breath, sounds, or all of the above.

HOW:

1. Assume a comfortable but alert upright position.
2. Gently bring your attention to the breath and note each inhalation and exhalation – without trying to change anything or breathe in any specific way.
3. When you notice your mind wandering (as it often does) gently bring your attention back to the breath and start again. At this point, you can choose to focus on a Mantra.

The meaning of Mantra: A mantra is a word, sound, or phrase repeated to aid in your concentration while meditating.

Modern day mantras:

"This too shall pass." (Endurance/Strength)
"I change my thoughts, I change my world." (Norman Vincent Peale)
"I love you, I'm sorry, Please forgive me and Thank you." (Hawaiian Prayer of Forgiveness, Ho'oponopono)
"Every day in every way I'm getting better and better." (Laura Silva)

Some favorite ancient mantras:

"Aum"|"Om" (Sanskrit/Hindu – means "It is")
"I AM that I AM" (Hebrew, "Ayer Asher Ayah" - God's name)
"Om Namah Shivaya"(Hindu, I honor the divinity within myself)
"Om Mani Padme Hum" (Buddhist, Hail the Buddha (Jewel) in the Lotus)
(Cartlett, 2015)

NOTE: It should be stated that mindfulness meditation while popular today is not a new practice. Meditation and meditative philosophy can lead to enlightenment and liberation from suffering. This has long been taught in Buddhism founded in the late 6th century B.C.E. by its founder Siddhartha Gautama.

Affirmation: *"Spirit have your way in my life."*

Self Control

The secret of success is learning how to use pain and pleasure instead of having pain and pleasure use you. If you don't, life controls you.
–Anthony Robbins

Thoughts of self-control visited me today and pulled me back from uttering sharp and cutting words. I AM grateful for introspective thinking, which prevented me from losing my composure.

Instead, I removed myself from the stimuli, changed my thoughts and attitude. This allowed me to reframe and shift my attention to more positive thoughts and positive deeds. I smile and my attitude changes to a friendlier one. I begin to breathe deeply and soon the freedom of averting a painful confrontation was averted.

In my retreat, I am relaxed and focused on more pleasant thoughts and things. I reach for my diary and become engrossed in my entry to further learn from what has happened.

I wrote: "Today, I learned how to have self-control, by speaking less and learning how to avoid destructive stimuli."

Sacred Practice: Self-control.

For one month, I will practice self-control in words, thoughts and action. I will write my daily observations in my diary and learn from them.

Affirmation: *I speak, think and act with humility and self-control.*

Forgiveness

Love Forgives All Errors
–Sharon Parris-Chambers

There is no forgiveness without genuine love. When we become love, we have the capacity to forgive.

Love removes the burden of toxic overload of waste thoughts that can easily be thrown out like rubbish.

Affirm: "I free my body and mind from negative, waste energy by taking in 'Prana,' 'Chi' clean energy which is channeled throughout my body."

You think positive thoughts, which eliminates negativity. If per chance you utter 'waste,' say immediately: "Cancel, Cancel, Cancel," or chant "I love you, I am sorry, please forgive me and thank you." (Ho'oponopono)

You are free to be a Divine being filled with light and love, the building blocks of the universe.

Sacred Practice:
When you become love, forgiveness is automatic. First, forgive yourself for the biggest mistake you have made in your life. Then forgive the smallest mistake. You can only forgive others when you have forgiven yourself. To forgive is to be Divine.

Visualize yourself seated across from someone who has done you wrong and speak your words of forgiveness to them. End with your own sincere prayer and the affirmation below.

Affirmation: *"I love you, I am sorry, please forgive me and thank you".* (Ho'oponopono).

Repeat as a mantra for 10 mins and often throughout the day every day. The prayer can help clean and delete negative thoughts and attitudes held deep within the subconscious. It returns one to a state of Divine love. Journal your experience.

I Believe in Me

I Believe in Me
–Sharon Parris-Chambers

Using the first person to express your consciousness is very empowering. You can use "I Believe in Me" as a tool for transformation. I believe in me and its manifestations are seen in my thoughts and actions. Yes, my attitude reflects who I AM. It reflects my belief in my skills and talents and goes one step further. The manifestation of my hopes, dreams and visions is played out in how I live my life, what I choose as my career, the people I surround myself with and ultimately my prosperity.

Learning to believe in yourself and your potentiality is the key to your success. Step out in trust and faith that the universe is working to guarantee your success.

Go for the gold! Don't look back. You are reaching forward to unchartered territory and this is good. You are growing spiritually and manifesting your destiny. When you step out on faith, you dig deep within and say, "I believe in Me!"

A successful outcome is assured.

Sacred Practice: Visualization Before Manifestation.

Using Visualization, project belief in yourself and your greatness. Sit back, take a deep breath and exhale forcefully. Repeat a few times.

Now, close your eyes and visualize (picture) yourself as the professional that you want to be or as the person that you want to be. Where you are respected and honored by others for the way you think and act. Go ahead and live your life from the Inside Out. See your success through visualization before manifestation.

Record your visualization in your diary.

Affirmation: *"I believe in me and my potentiality. I AM not afraid of my greatness."*

Freedom

I AM Free to be a conscious being
filled with light and love.
−*Sharon Parris-Chambers*

Can you truly say that your limiting beliefs and actions are not retarding your progress?

Today, you can say and believe: "I AM Free to be a conscious being filled with light and love. I AM Free to be me. It is time that I find my authentic self and be directed from within, freeing myself from group think and the tribe."

Yes, I am a member of the human family, which in the metaphysical sense is One Self. Yet, I am uniquely me. I am manifesting my destiny, as the secret person of the heart. I AM transformed in mind, body and spirit. I AM Free to be me.

Practice: **Pranic Healing Meditation.**

Go to Youtube.com and search for: *The Twin Hearts Meditation* by Master Stephen Co. Learn how to bring heart and crown chakras in alignment. Experience the exhilaration of divine healing. (Cok Sui, 2017)

Use the "Om" mantra. In between "Oms" please concentrate on the Silence, do not be afraid of it. When practiced regularly with focus and concentration, you can reach an awakened state of awareness.

Affirmation: *I AM free to be me.*

I AM Light and I AM Love.
–Sharon Parris-Chambers

Who am I? I am a being of light and love. No longer will I hide behind anyone or anything. My essence reflects the Divine Universe, the source of all light and life.

I will let my light shine so bright that all who gaze upon me will know my source and embrace the same life force that resides within them.

I AM Light and I AM Love. Light is love and Love is light. The two are one and the same, sometimes expressed differently but still the same.

Sacred Practice:
Sit quietly, breathing deeply, inhale and exhale. Repeat until you are very relaxed. See yourself surrounded by the power and transparence of golden light. Now become the Light. It is your original source. Imagine the sun, the stars, and their energies. Earth reflects the universe. The stars that collided, recreating themselves into new universes are in us. We are starlight. See it, believe it and become it. Remain in this state of consciousness for as long as you can.

Next, see yourself as love (See the color Rose reflective of the Heart Chakra the source of love and intuition.) Feel a vibration of warm energy surging through your being. I am speaking of Divine love, or universal love, which encompasses humanity as One Heart and One

Self, yes, One Love. This love is not dependent on anyone or anything; it is the fullness and the totality of all there is. Open your heart center to this energy. See it, Feel it and Become it.

Practice this every day and soon you will be filled with Light and Love, transforming and transcending from your physical essence into a spiritual one. Now share your Divine Love with every being on the planet, one heart at a time.

Affirmation: *I AM Light: I Feel it, See it and Become it.*

I AM My Breath
–Sharon Parris-Chambers

I AM the breath of life, the constitution of the universe. There is nothing closer to me than my breath. I honor it. My breath is my beloved; I am spoken for. There is no other love as true and wonderful. There is no trauma, no drama. There is predictability and reliability. I AM one with creation through the breath of life. And so it is, Ashe.

Sacred Practice: **Breath of Fire & Five Tibetan Rites of Rejuvenation.** Sitting comfortably with your back straight. Begin to do the 'Breath of Fire' exercise. (Pranayama) It is rapid breathing like a dog panting. Do these 100 times, forcibly. How do you feel? If there is discomfort, stop and relax. As you continue to do this exercise, you will strengthen your lungs enabling it to take in more air. Now, continue with your activities or rest and enjoy this feeling of wellbeing and freedom.
Thereafter breathe naturally and deeply from the diaphragm.
Listen to the 'Five Tibetan Rites of Rejuvenation' CD on YouTube and begin to learn how to strengthen your core and protect against disease. Research shows that Monks have used these rites to increase their vitality and longevity.

My dear friend, a writer and yogini, Rachel Citrin is over 90 years of age. She is alert, flexible and practices these sacred rites daily. Rachel says it is important to "keep moving." She taught me the "Five Tibetan Rites of Rejuvenation" exercise in Jamaica as part of a writing workshop, which was combined with breathing exercises and prayer, in preparation to communicate with the Muse or Sage within. Since then, I have taught over 15 persons the Tibetan Rites of Rejuvenation. Rachel uses the positive energy and flexibility from the Tibetan Rites to fuel her movement in Danza de Alma classes in Mexico or where ever in the world she travels. Journal your experiences.

Affirmation: *I AM Love and Life. (Repeat Often)*

Healing

Healing of the nation begins with me.
–Sharon Parris-Chambers

The healing of the nation which is central to healing the world begins with you. Change must begin with 'me,' and every individual, one heart at a time.

Beginning with this premise and understanding is the first step to bringing the change you seek.

As a values facilitator, I assisted in staging Train the Trainer Workshops for teachers in values education using the Living Values Education Program (LVEP) in Jamaica from 2003-2007.

The lessons begin with Peace, followed by Love, Respect and ten other values: Honesty, Simplicity, Cooperation, Happiness, Humility, Forgiveness, Tolerance, Responsibility, Freedom and Unity. The reason that we begin training with peace is that, Peace is our essential physical state; we are beings of peace. What is Peace? It is more than an absence of war. Dadi Janki, Spiritual leader of the Brahma Kumaris and supporter of values education is now aged 102. She has asked us to live our lives from the *Inside out,* the title of one of her books, focused on five values: peace, love, purity, happiness and divine truth. (Janki, 2003) If we see the world with true clarity, taking responsibility for our actions, and living our positive values, it truly could help make the world a better place.

Begin to heal yourself through daily meditation and reflection. Add affirmations to help you focus on changing your attitude and behaviors.

Sacred Practice:

Develop a positive mental attitude (PMA). What is your attitude? It is what you are thinking and doing. Change wrong thinking before the thought manifests physically. "Cancel" or change limiting thoughts from manifesting or taking control of your conscious thoughts. Dr Wayne Dyer remind us *"Change your thoughts -change your life."* (Dyer, 2007) After you practice being aware of your conscious thoughts, you will then be ready to tackle unconscious thoughts. Through the regular practice of visualization and meditation you can reduce and remove limiting beliefs.

Affirmation: *Healing the nation begins with me.*

Joy

True joy is achieved living one day at a time.
–Sharon Parris-Chambers

A well-known and beloved modern Guru of our time, Sadghuru Jaggi Vasudev, speaks on the subject of bliss: *"Fear, anger, resentment and stress are poisons you create in your mind. If you take charge of your mind you can create a chemistry of blissfulness."*

Joy is an experiential value so let us experience it instead of speaking about it. Let joy become you, overwhelm you, so that you remain in a state of blissfulness. In this way, you bring harmony to your mind, body and spirit. Living in this state, you prevent disease and discomfort from infecting your own being. You attract persons of like kind and impact humanity through sending out your blissful vibrations.

Sacred Practice: Create a space where you are free from worry and daily concerns. Relax and enjoy the feeling of weightlessness, freedom and happiness. Now, take a few deep breaths. Visualize yourself in your favorite place to relax - a meadow, river or a garden. See yourself happy, carefree and enjoying each moment. Visualize yourself in this scenario and internalize these words:

> **Visualization - Joy.**
> Create a space where you are free from worry and daily concerns. Relax and enjoy the feeling of weightlessness, freedom and

happiness. Now, take a few deep breaths. Visualize yourself in your favorite place of relaxation, such as a meadow, river or garden. See yourself happy, carefree and enjoying each moment of the day. Visualize yourself in this scenario and internalize these words:

"I am happy and carefree, enjoying this moment in time by the river. The water is clear and cool on this hot summer day. I feel like jumping in, but I will start by putting my feet in first. Aah, that feels nice, it is heavenly!" Sitting down, I promise myself that I will take time out to enjoy this moment at the river bank. A flock of gray and white birds fly overhead, making some 'squawky' sounds. They line up in a wondrous V formation. I look up at the azure blue sky and smile. Being in nature is having a positive and calming effect on me.

I see a set of steps leading to the beach. I rise and begin to follow the path which is lined by beautiful ginger red flowers, birds of paradise sunset red and orange hanging flowers, and Thumburgia purple delicate flowers on a meandering vine. And there are various species of ferns and orchids. I descend, while savoring every moment. I smile and tell myself that I am so fortunate to be enjoying this quiet moment in time. I approach the bottom. I looked around and saw the same kind of lush colorful beauty around me. I arrive at sea level and immediately ran to the pink sand beach and jump into the coolest, most refreshing water! I swam for what seemed like 15 minutes.

I enjoy the moment, returning to my place of rest. It is there I saw a few persons walking towards me while I frolic in the water. A man and woman walk up and say "hello". I replied "hello, how are you?" The woman said, "enjoying the beauty of this perfect day." "Have you seen any starfish, stingray or jellyfish today?" "Yes, I have seen some starfish, but luckily no jellyfish today." Like me, they sat and stared out to sea.

Soon, I felt the urge to begin walking back alone, so that I could enjoy the beautiful landscape, flora and fauna. "I will be leaving now, it was a pleasure meeting you both," I said, and slowly walked away.
-Guided Meditation by Sharon Parris-Chambers.

Repeat the above in the 'third person' as though you are a coach. This approach will have a profound impact by rewriting negative feelings with positive ones in your subconscious mind. Begin with the following:

"You are happy and carefree, enjoying this moment in time down by the river… Repeat the above scenario.

I return to this conscious now moment, refreshed and rejuvenated. I smile easily and know that my joy is in each conscious moment spent being aware of nature around me, paying attention to people, places and things. I know intuitively that everything will work out in the fullness of time. If you must force something to happen, perhaps it won't happen. Instead, just step back and allow the Universe to help you or orchestrate the desired outcome.

Affirmation: *I remove the mist of my mind and find joy.*

Breath Consciousness

Eye Am My One Breath Cosmos, Breathing
and Pulsating Consciously Forever.
–Desmond Green

Live in the Now with every breath you take.
–Sharon Parris-Chambers

Each day when I awake, I realize that that today is the first day of the rest of my life. It gives me a renewed sense of hope! When I live in the now my life expresses me and I awaken to a new reality, one thought at a time. I remember that there is no time for lamenting. Life is calling humanity to express its greatest potential with every breath it takes.

Having learned and practiced Traffic Control of the mind from the Brahma Kumaris, I have found it to be a powerful self-management tool to harness the mind and to keep it focused. Overtime, I have found the technique to be relevant and effective in focusing my thoughts and actions. I invite you to join me in this sacred practice.

Sacred Practice:
Sit in a quiet place. Every hour, engage in traffic control of the mind, resolve that nothing will keep you from quieting your mind for the next 5 minutes. Stop thinking and focus on a mantra, such as: "I AM that I AM", "Peace be still" or "I am Love and Light." Do this for 5 minutes. Then return to what you were doing.

You may also choose specific times to retreat to your Inner Temple such as 6:00 a.m., 9:00 a.m., Noon, 3:00 p.m. and 6:00 p.m. to establish the practice.

It is interesting to note that the ancients have identified certain times as more fortuitous than others having strong impacts on energetic vibrations.

Quiet the mind, focus on your Mantra, a Candle or your Breath. Relax and then Record your thoughts. This practice when applied regularly will help you learn to focus your thoughts and actions, enabling you to become the master of your destiny.

Affirmation: *I live In the Now moment of eternity.*

You are Breathdancing ™ with Prana energy this moment.
–Sharon Parris-Chambers

Breathdancing ™ is using the breath to sustain the body, removing blockages with forceful breathing and recognizing that you are your breath. Awareness of the breath informs the quality of your life. Conscious breathers have no fear or lack. Their attitude is a magnet for success.

The philosophy of my mentor Dr Wayne Dyer fits nicely here: *"The more you see yourself as what you'd like to become, and act as if what you want is already there, the more you'll activate those dormant forces that will collaborate to transform your dream into your reality."* (Dyer W., 1997)

You live in the now, the ever-present moment. You learn to take one day at a time and truly live in the moment. You are a Divine being having an earthly experience. Open your heart to One Love – universal love and acceptance.

Sacred Practice:
Breathe deeply now, take in the breath of life. You are breathdancing ™ using Prana energy. Inhale and Exhale. Relax and follow the breath… Follow the breath. You are going on a journey, to discover the inner you. This is a place where you sometimes forget to visit. You are going there now, to your Temple of Inner Peace. Using your thoughts, feelings, sensory perceptions visualize yourself inside the place called YOU.

Turn your intention within to your inner Self. In this place called YOU, where you can be yourself. There is no one to criticize or hurt YOU. Relax and say with meaning "I love me," "I love every part of my body." There is nothing to fear, go ahead, and Smile, Relax now. You are a Divine being full of love, light, energy and vibration. See yourself filled with love, light and laughter.

Breathe deeply now, take in the breath of life, you are breathdancing ™ using Prana energy. Inhale and exhale. Relax and follow the breath.

Affirmation: *I am breathing and morphing into the conscious awareness of One Self.*

Insource before you Outsource. Look
within to your source of all good.
−Sharon Parris-Chambers

Where would you be without your breath? Inhale and exhale take in the breath of life.

This is your Insource which is breathing you, nourishing you, living life through you and expressing your divinity.

Insource before you outsource. Look within. Take inventory of Self, Inhale and exhale. Take in the breath of life. Center yourself in the quiet of your inner Temple.

Sacred Practice:
When you reinforce your sacred life practice daily, you manifest your destiny and enter Paradise. Choose the right time to mediate daily. Follow up at that time every day and evening. Find yourself a quiet space and start breathing deeply. Take cleansing breaths, Deep, Deep breaths that brings in the Life Energy; use that life energy to create your world, not one of fear, but one of positivity, success and prosperity.

Sit in Zazen, quiet contemplative meditation. Use a mantra of your choice. You determine how long to sit based on your intuition.

Journal your experience.

Affirmation: *I AM my Divine Self.*

Stay connected to Chi or Prana
through breath consciousness.
–Sharon Parris-Chambers

Chi or Prana is universal breath consciousness. You connect to it through deep breathing, through your meditations, through your thoughts. Take in life energy and exhale unwanted feelings the more life energy you take in, the more positive, and healthy you become.

You may receive Chi or Prana energy through hands on application of Reiki healing, Pranic healing and other forms of energy healing. Holistic Massage is a healing system that can harness and apply Chi energy for relaxation and wellbeing.

Experiment with Chi energy stay connected and in tune with universal consciousness.

Sacred Practice: When you reinforce your sacred life practice daily, you manifest your destiny and enter Paradise. Choose the opportune time to meditate daily. Find a quiet space and start breathing deeply. Take cleansing breaths, Deep, Deep breaths that recharges the Life Energy. Use that life energy to create your world, not of fear, but positivity, success and prosperity.

For Reiki practitioners: When in a relaxed state, apply Reiki energy to create feelings of wellbeing and balance.

Affirmation: *My breath is my beloved.*
Journal your experiences.

SPIRITUAL DEVELOPMENT

"We are not human beings in search of a spiritual experience. We are spiritual beings immersed in a human experience." — Wayne Dyer

Pacify Your Restless Mind

How does one find peace while coexisting with such a restless mind? The answer lies in emptying the mind of useless clutter to find stillness, the Presence of God consciousness.
–Sharon Parris-Chambers

Mind is what it is. A Conduit of impulses, images and feelings transmitted to your conscious self.

In my book *Poetry from the Rose of Sharon: Divine thoughts for Living Well*, I wrote:

"Truth seekers who really want to see, to break through the illusion and see with clarity, turn to seeing with the heart. It never lies. It knows the soul's journey and is your internal spirit guide." (Parris-Chambers, 2011) This quote takes us into another realm of existence, moving from a mental construct and thinking our way through life to the heart's core of feeling and knowing from the soul's perspective.

There is no room for intellectualizing, using your mind to avoid dealing directly with life's situations. The mind is so overactive, it is always thinking, weaving a tangled web that entraps you.

It is TIME for the 'restless monkey' mind to STOP.

Sacred Practice: Practice Traffic Control of your thoughts, stopping at fixed points throughout the day to quiet the mind. Take 5 minutes daily for 30 days to practice Traffic Control of your thoughts. At regular intervals 9:00 a.m., 12 Noon, 3:00 p.m. and 6:00 p.m. STOP what you are doing and Clear your conscious mind. Say: *"I need clarity now, I will deal with all other thoughts later."* This is a time to be one with nature. No thinking, just being. Or you may wish to focus on a mantra, such as: *I am Love, I am Peace, I am well in mind, body and spirit or I AM.*

At the end of 5 minutes, write your reflections in your journal. You would have done Traffic Control for 20 minutes each day. At the end of 30 days read the entire month's activities and see how much progress you have made. You may choose to increase or decrease the time and days for reflection. Only you know your needs.

A worthy observation: "It bewilders that we can find time for everything else, but the nourishment of our mind." You Can Do This!

AFFIRMATION: *I empty my mind of useless clutter.*
(Repeat throughout the day.) *I Can Do This!*

Just for a minute, lose yourself, get out of your conscious mind; then you can discover who you really are.
–Sharon Parris-Chambers

It is essential in this fast-paced world that we develop coping mechanisms to slow the 'monkey mind' jumping from one thing to another without any closure. Taking time for reflection, meditation and even day-dreaming yields significant results. One must take time for personal retreats.

Spend a day being in and interacting with nature. Sit under a tree or hug a tree, reflect on your feelings and reactions; just be in the moment. You will be rejuvenated and renewed. Use a journal to capture your experiences.

In a past retreat, students were instructed to go out, find a tree, hug it and interact with it in some way. They returned to the group and shared their experiences. A woman with cancer and nerve issues went and sat under a guanabana (soursop tree). It turned out that was exactly the fruit she needed, unknown to her, to treat her ailments. The overall results of this retreat were so profound and insightful that I am encouraged now to ask you to repeat this practice.

Sacred Practice:
Take 15 to 30 minutes daily to lose yourself in nature, vacate your conscious mind and find your true ego-less self. If at first you cannot empty the mind, just persist by walking in nature and being enthralled by the things around you. Refrain from judgment. Just be. Next,

find a tree, hug it and begin to interact with it. Allow yourself to be open and free to receive all impulses and vibrations. Journal your experiences.

AFFIRMATION: *I AM That I AM.*

When we are like water, nothing stops our flow.
–Sharon Parris-Chambers

Find a way over, under or around the obstacle. Water is fluid, flexible and changes its form to accommodate any object. It is a primary source of life, as important as the sun is on earth. But do you understand the hidden power of water?

Water has tremendous powers of healing. For centuries, people have used natural spas, a body of water known for healing and rejuvenation. Through practice you can discover how bathing in natural spring or ocean water can change your life. Examples are the healing attributes of thalassotherapy (ocean water baths), balneotherapy (thermal baths) and hydrotherapy (water spa treatments).

In the final analysis, *we are energy and vibration at our core.* Like water, we can find a way around any obstacle through the vibration of love. Stay in love and you will remain fluid, in alignment with the Universe. Ideas that you are seeking and solutions to problems offer themselves freely. Let love be a factor in your life as water is to the ocean.

Sacred Practice: Go to the ocean or river today. Immerse yourself in water, relax and be one with it. Become water. Fluid, buoyant and unbounded.

Nature's water source is best. Just focus on the present moment. Watch the ebb and flow of nature before you.

Take note of the energy and vibration of water and be like water. It is you and you are water; it comprises 70% of your body. Take note of how you feel during and after immersion. Write your observations in your journal. This is your journey, make the best of it.

Affirmations: *I AM water and nothing stops my flow.*
I live in the now moment of the eternal flow of life.

> *When we remain as our intrinsic selves, we*
> *stand firmly in our Truth as Divine beings.*
> *–Sharon Parris-Chambers*

The idea of the human being comes under repeated attack by the ego within and without. Who is really being attacked? Is it the Self that is being attacked? Or is it the personality? These parts of the Self are blocking us from a deeper more meaningful experience of the Higher Self. Each perceived problem that arises is replaced by the next, resulting in an endless spiral of so-called problems. These constructs appear to be important, but they are not.

Stay in the beingness of who you are as a Presence. When you empty the mind, you will feel a vibration that will replace belief. It is the essence of the Soul also known as the Presence.

The mind can become like a lion. Do not let the lion pounce and devour you.

Resist the impressions of the mind, the urgings and mindless chatter. *Pacify the mind by retreating from it.* Stay in the present moment.

Can the disguises of the mind offer anything to the heart? Can it offer anything to the Self? The mind must serve the Self. Merge with your Self as a sentient and conscious being.

Sacred Practice: Prayer: 'Rid me of Ego'

Divine Spirit of my higher Self, rid me of ego and the feeling of separation. Merge me with you, who are my own Self. And so it is.

-Mooji

Affirmation: I am my transcendent Self

Take wellness out of your mind by renewing your Spirit.
—Sharon Parris-Chambers

The mind is a mental construct which observes and approves our conscious experience. It is broken down into id- ego- superego and these facets, according to psychiatrist Sigmund Freud, help define personality, attitude and behavior.

You must go outside of your conscious mind to renew the Spirit. It cannot be done from within the divisions of the human mind.

To be well in mind, body and spirit, one must take wellness out of the mind and place it into a spiritual domain, an enlightened place to facilitate the renewal of the Spirit. When this is committed to daily practice fueled with right intention, spiritual renewal will take place.

Sacred Practice: Universal Oneness.
Begin and end the day totally in alignment with the universe. Let every thought that fire into your consciousness and every Divine action be in harmony with Peace and Love. Do this upon awaking, enter meditation using the sound of creation "AAH (as in Hallelujah) in your sacred place for a minimum of 15 minutes. During the day, actively monitor your thoughts, and in the evening, begin meditation using the "OHM" – the sound of creation for 15 minutes. Then, relax into your being as a peaceful soul. In this state of spiritual wellness, the whole being experiences renewal and transformation.

Affirmation: *I AM one with the universe.*

I AM *reborn every day in divine consciousness*
–Sharon Parris-Chambers

Every night I go to sleep with my old self, and its idiosyncrasies, but every morning I awake in divine consciousness through meditation and perception as a Divine being. Only then can I ward off physical and emotional dis-ease.

On arising, I immediately call on my divine angels (within) to guide and protect me from my own destructive ego, circular negative thinking and restless mind. This frees me by allowing access to the realm of divinity within my own being. I become open, trusting, forgiving, pure in mind and spirit. I vibrate at the speed of light and attract others of the same spirit.

Sacred Practice: Reborn Every Day.
Enter the gap, space between thoughts, hold a consciousness of quietude and relaxation. Enter meditation and empty your mind. There in the quiet space, unload your worries and concerns. Begin by giving thanks for what you are to receive. Ask your questions and remain alert for answers. When you are ready, return to the world of your creation.

Take the Pledge: One Love Call to Action & Pledge ~ www.facebook. com/OneLoveCallToActionPledge

"I Pledge to Love, Forgive, Trust and Respect Myself and Others. In so doing, I heal Myself and (my country) with One Love One Heart at a Time."

Live your dream through Faith in your Greatness
–Sharon Parris-Chambers
Tribute to Dr Martin Luther King, Jr. January 18, 2016

Manifest your Destiny by Living your Dream, through Faith in your Greatness, NOT your weakness. You are a Divine being, uniquely designed in mind, body and spirit to reflect the source of your greatness, which is God (Divine Universe). Live the Life of your Creation NOW!

You are a creator, whether you believe it or not, it is still true. You are responsible for each thought you create, once they burst into your consciousness. These become your reality. Therefore, it is important to be conscious of your every thought. When you daydream, your thoughts take you over temporarily, you become unawares of your present state. These thoughts can create either positive or negative outcomes.

When I speak of Conscious living, which is the opposite of daydreaming, I am calling you to stand in your power as a Creator, as a god or goddess. With this mindset, you are fully aware of your decisions and you ACT in your capacity as a CREATOR.

Sacred Practice: Reflect on Dr Martin Luther King's "*I have a dream speech*". (King, 1963)

-Highlight the moral values in the speech and then identify your own moral values. Journal your thoughts on this subject and review for an entire week.

Affirmation: *I live my dream one day at a time.*

Let life Touch You
–Sharon Parris-Chambers

Let life touch you. Do not build a wall around yourself. You are not an island. A Divine being lives in the moment and learns how to transcend the vicissitudes of life which ebbs and flows like the sea. However, you can harness the mind which wanders, gets cluttered with mindless, wasteful thoughts.

Take time today to still the mind, which can be done through reflection and meditation. It really is possible. Begin to do this in the mornings before sunrise and at sunset. In reflection, one does more than just daydream. One thinks on actions and behaviors with a resolve to improve self. Meditation is an attempt to still the thoughts and noise of the mind. When the mind is still, you will hear and feel the new impulses. You will be guided so that answers that you have been seeking will appear seemingly from out of nowhere.

Sacred Practice:
Sit quietly today during daybreak and again at sunrise. Relax, deep inhale, deep exhale; Relax. Repeat. Light a candle and watch its flame; this is to teach you to focus your eyes. While looking at the candle, begin now to focus on your quiet rhythmic breathing; Relax. Allow your thoughts to come and go. Do not focus on them. This is your quiet time to empty the mind of its worries, fears and anxieties. After a while, you will begin to feel light, empty and joyful.

Do this every day for 30 days and record your experiences. Breakthrough ideas for projects and brilliant ideas will surface into your consciousness.

Continue daily reflection and meditation, then watch your life begin to transform into the life which you have always dreamed.

Regular Meditation is a necessary part of your journey, so open your mind and Let Life Touch You!

Affirmation: *I love the life I live and I live the life I love.*

Let the Real You Stand Up
–Sharon Parris-Chambers

DO NOT hesitate to Re-Invent yourself any time you choose to be the You that You Really, Really Want to Be. You are a representation of the Divine Universe. It is Time to Live your Truth.

What do you gain by marginalizing your abilities?

As of today, prepare to embrace You as a brilliant star, a reflection of the dynamic universe of which You are a part. We do not have time to keep searching to find ourselves. We can begin to say, 'The soul which was lost is now found.' Pledge to remain in conscious awareness of who you are. Accept your Greatness and move on.

The author of *Anam Cara: Your Soul Friend and Bridge to Enlightenment and Creativity*, Dr Glenville Ashby says, *"Friendship is a profound bond, a heart-to-heart connection that takes time to nurture. It's rooted in the soul, not to be constrained by time or space."* (Ashby, 2016) Evoke your Anam Cara, your Spiritual Guide to stand by you, whenever you need guidance and protection.

Sacred Practice:
During your quiet time, visualize yourself stepping up to do the things that you believe you cannot do. Feel the pain, feel the doubt and anxiety and then say, "If Eleanor Roosevelt can do what she thinks she cannot do, then so can I". "Yes, I can do all things through the I AM presence or Divine Spirit within me."

Reflect on the following Quote: "*You must do the thing you think you cannot do.*"

- Eleanor Roosevelt, U.S. first lady, diplomat and activist

AFFIRMATION: *The I AM Presence in me can do all things.*

I Live my dream and sometimes my dream lives me.
    −Sharon Parris-Chambers

"I am a dreamer who constantly dreams. The dream of Life mocks my reality and pushes me further in search of my awakening." By Sharon Parris-Chambers

My awakening is the flip side of life sometimes called reality. The sleep/wake stage outside of this dream state mimics reality.

The following quote from *The Prophet*, Kahlil Gibran refers to his dreams "And his soul cried out to them, and he said: "Sons of my ancient mother, you riders of the tides, how often have you sailed in my dreams. And now you come in my awakening, which is my deeper dream. Ready am I to go, and my eagerness with sails full set awaits the wind." (Gibran, 1923)

The Poet awakens from his wishful dream for the mariner's return. As the ship comes in He sees this as his 'deeper dream' and his longing to travel.

Is your consciousness your deeper dream or awakening?

Sacred Practice:
Practice quiet sitting and reflection daily with the goal of emptying your mind. Begin after arising, find a quiet place, sit and focus on your breath. You will begin to feel relaxed. Sit in this relaxed state, as images or distractions enter your mind, dismiss them. Remain in this state of quietude for as long as you can.

Repeat, during the day and in the evening before bed. After a three-week period, you will begin to form a pattern. This practice will begin to help you live life from an awakened state of consciousness.

"Life will begin to live you and you can truly say "I live my dream every day and sometimes my dream lives me." This means your dream and your reality ARE one.

Affirmation: *I live life and life lives me.*

Awaken the God or Goddess in you
−Sharon Parris-Chambers

You reflect the universe, a reflection of the stars that collide to create universes and galaxies. It is time to Awaken the God or Goddess residing in you, today! Do you sometimes awaken with doubt and fear about your future? Has it worn you out until you just got sick and tired of feeling this way? Are you looking for another way of experiencing life that leaves you feeling exhilarated, light and free?

You are who you have been looking for. Accept your greatness. There is no need to belittle or look down on yourself.

Sacred Practice:
It is time to try something different. Begin to breathe in the breath of life as a Divine being with full confidence. Feel the breath surging in and through you. Now, relax into your being. Your breath is your constitution for living. You owe nothing to anyone but love. Your reason for being is to find your dharma, purpose for living. Before you can do this, though, you should know who you are.

Absorb the following words of Marianne Williamson, a spiritual thought leader and poet: *"Our deepest fear is not that we are inadequate. Our deepest fear is that we are powerful beyond measure. It is our light, not our darkness that most frightens us. We ask ourselves, 'Who am I to be brilliant, gorgeous, talented, fabulous?' Actually, who are you not to be? You are a child of God. Your playing small does not serve the world. There is nothing enlightened about shrinking so that other people won't feel insecure around you. We are all meant to shine, as children do."* (Williamson, 1992)

Affirmation: *I am the Universe and the Universe is in me.*

Choose to Stop suffering now by shifting your Memory and Imagination to a more positive space.
—Sharon Parris-Chambers

Today marks the first day of the rest of your life. Live your life, exert your positive intentions or Let life live you and exert its unknown intentions upon you.

Stop suffering by removing ALL limitations from your mind and imagination. You are what you think about every moment. Vision yourself the way you want to be. Shift - Focus and re-Connect to a new Conscious and Visual image of yourself.

You can actively choose to stop suffering in your mind and imagination NOW! Leave yesterday in the dustbin of eternity. Suffering is NOT a way of life. Recite the mantra *Ho'oponopono* (*I love you, I am sorry, please forgive me and thank you*) to clean and delete all negative thoughts and images. Transforming the personality takes time. So be patient. Begin to consciously cancel and delete negative thoughts and eventually you will become more positive, and harmonious.

Choose today to live your life on purpose, with passion and intention.

Sacred Practice: Mirror Image.
Stand in front of the mirror and speak to your mirror image. Cross your hands over your heart and look into your eyes. *Say: "I love me and I honor me." "I will never allow anyone to hurt or abuse me." "I will never give up on me." "I love my life and enjoy being alive."*

Then turn it around as if you are the Coach speaking and say: *"I love you and I honor you." "I will never allow anyone to hurt or abuse you." I will never give up on you." Love the life you live and enjoy yourself."* Smile and visualize the feeling of being loved by your parents, friends and family. Enjoy these vibrations. Repeat as often as necessary.

Affirmation: *I choose to Live Life to the Fullest*!

Shift – Focus and Connect to the Universe
–Sharon Parris-Chambers

The phrase Shift – Focus and Connect to the Universe came to me during my meditation around the time writing of my first book, *"Poetry from the Rose of Sharon: Divine Thoughts and Inspirations for Living Well"* (Parris-Chambers, 2011).

It is from this experience that I devised this mental exercise. It has proven to be a useful sacred practice to connect with Divine consciousness.

When life seems to get you down, don't fret, don't curse. Shift, Focus and Connect to the universe.

Don't fight, don't explode, just Shift, Focus and Connect to the universe. Remove yourself from your mental struggles and pay attention to life. You may use this as a coping mechanism to manage life's situations. Begin to Connect to nature and life around you.

Reflect on this during the sacred practice: *'Am I responsible for all my thoughts and experiences or just some of them?'*

Sacred Practice: Inhale-Focus-Connect.
Use this simple practice to Connect to Chi energy:
Inhale – Focus – Connect – Ask your question.
Exhale - Focus – Connect
Inhale – Focus – Connect – Ask your question.
Exhale – Focus - Connect

Repeat for ten rounds and relax. You may choose to stay with the first question or ask new questions.

Just shift your attention from negativity to a positive mental attitude.

Focus your mind and connect to the universe.
Do it every time and be blessed with new energy.
Look ahead and feel the surge.

Be free from stress; Create new synergy.
Just Shift – Focus and Connect to the universe.

Inhale – Focus – Connect – Ask your question.
Exhale - Focus – Connect
Inhale – Focus – Connect – Ask your question.
Exhale – Focus - Connect

Just Shift your attention away from worry and fear, connect to Divine consciousness.

Focus your mind and connect to the universe.
Wake up to a new reality of universal oneness.
When you Shift – Focus and Connect to the universe.

Affirmation: *I experience life as it is.*

Who am I?

Sages, mystics, bards, philosophers, poets and truth-seekers the world over have explored the inner self to find the answer to the question "Who am I?

Today I ask you to explore the same question. The time is now to know who you truly are. Sometimes the inner person or the inner Sage is elusive. You must persist, and you will find that which you seek. The journey requires perseverance.

It is a daily exploration of quiet reflection and seeking. If you persist, you will find all the answers that you seek.

Who am I? Spirit animates me and I awaken to my divine potentiality. Let this Spirit permeate you today. Remove your ego consciousness and discover who you truly are!

Sacred Practice: Sit in a quiet place, begin to settle yourself. If questions arise in your mind, say "I will deal with these later." Take a deep breath, hold, exhale. Repeat as often as you need until you are relaxed. Now, begin to follow your breath until you are one with it. Introduce your question(s) and allow the answers to come forward as impulses or clear responses within your being. Listen to that quiet voice or the loud response that you have been waiting for. Accept these spiritual gifts and give thanks silently. Continue to ask other questions, or just relax into your being as energy and vibration.

Affirmation: *I AM a being of limitless potentiality.*

Your ancient future is expressing you in the now.
–Sharon Parris-Chambers

You are the essence of life and greatness. Your genome holds the secret of your timeless history. Your ancient future is expressing you in the now. At this very moment, you are the sum of your past, present and future.

Human beings are unique among creatures, they possess a fascinating capacity to advance their emotional intelligence. You are unique, having the capacity to reflect, imagine and impact your experience with your thoughts and lucid dreams.

Practice living in the now and enhance your spiritual development through your imagination and faculties. You only have today to challenge yourself. Move one step closer to your Divinity by expressing your ancient future in the now.

Sacred Practice: *Heart of the Rose*
Find a quiet place to spend a minimum of ten minutes for this sacred practice. Reflect on the *Heart of the Rose*. Review the *Heart of the Rose* Meditation in the Appendix to recall the details. The benefits of this practice will lure you to repeat this thousand-year-old practice often. When practiced with full intent you become more energetic, revitalized and revivified.

Affirmation: *I am energy and vibration.*

*The universe of your Inner Space awaits
your exploration and awareness that you can
launch Peace and Love throughout Universes
and Galaxies from right here on Earth.*
−Sharon Parris-Chambers

Live life from the Inside Out. There is a universe in your Inner Space awaiting your acknowledgement and exploration. When will you make the shift from external Livity[1] to internal. It is time to move from external reference to internal reference, to live life from your Divine Temple of inner peace.

Your genome knows your greatness, as does the trillions of cells in your body, which beckons you to recognize your greatness. These trillions of cells are only outnumbered by the sands on the seashore and stars in the sky. Your cells are a microcosm of the universe. Humans have created everything with their thoughts from the airplane to the xylophone.

Twenty-first century beings are creating spacecrafts for human outer space visits and will one day replace travel as we know it. Whether you believe it or not, Inventors – past and present - are not unlike us. The difference is their willingness to think outside the box, to be intrepid and determined to realize their goals.

Are you creating the successful life that you envision? Or are you just imagining your life without adding the Passion, Drive and Creativity necessary to move it from a dream into Reality?

---

[1] Livity is a holistic spiritual lifestyle often referred to by Rastafari.

We are the ones that we have been waiting for. Do not throw AWAY YOUR POTENTIAL. Begin to live from the Inside Out without fear. You will begin to smile again and live the life of your dreams.

Sacred Practice: Choose a Practice from the Appendix.

Journal your experiences.

Affirmation: *I AM the Universe and the Universe is in me.*

Are you Moving from Independence to Interdependence?
–Sharon Parris-Chambers

Human beings have an independent spirit. This speaks to the universal push from within the Divine being, which seeks to express at the cellular level. In the face of diversity and population explosions in some parts of the world, we maintain our individuality.

And although we are members of the global family we nevertheless grow in consciousness and self-awareness. Innately, we are unique and transitioning from independence to interdependence as a necessary rite of passage.

We must focus on making the world a better place. This means relying on, working, collaborating and communicating with and Not fighting with each other.

We must live in peace and harmony.

In this regard our aim is unification of our shared interests and goals as one human family. The African principle Ubuntu teaches "I am because we all are." This is a great way of showcasing cultural and universal diversity. Let us look for opportunities to celebrate the human family one nation at a time through music, dance, entertainment, poetry, prose, language, literature, debates, colloquium and other shared projects.

Let us begin by honoring our own bodies as the temple of the Most High from the cellular level by keeping our house (body) clean, free from negative energies and foreign substances. Honoring our families, our communities, our country; then move outward to sharing the joys of peace, love, respect and unity with humanity.

Sacred Practice: Find a quiet space for meditation. Sit quietly, begin to breathe deeply until you are relaxed. Thank your ancestors, your angels, sages and guides for their love and protection. Then, Visualize the earth in front of you as a small ball. Bless the earth with peace and love. See Divine white light surrounding the earth. Hold that intention and vision as long as you can. Then say your individual prayer and end the meditation when you are ready.

Affirmation: *I AM one with humanity.*

Live Life as though you were given a second chance to manifest your destiny.
—Sharon Parris-Chambers

I have heard many times people reminisce on their lives and wish for another chance to re-create their lives. When we hold on to these limiting thoughts, we waste time living in the past.

Have you ever been face to face with a life or death decision? What do you do? Do you have support systems that you can rely on or are you going it alone? These are important questions to contemplate before the appointed time arises.

Life offers no guarantees. It requires that you live in accordance with universal laws that honor your body temple and Earth Mother (Gaia). You live 24/7 in your body. So, it is important to take care of your body (house). Get your house in order. Get regular annual medical checks. Eat ethical raw foods & drink clean, spring water as often as possible. Detox the body system regularly and exercise.

Your commitment to live the conscious and holistic lifestyle in the now is all there is.

Sacred Practice: Write your Gratitude List
Upon awakening daily, write down at least 10 things that you are grateful for. At the end of the week review all entries and enjoy the

feeling of great joy, fulfillment and prosperity that humility and gratitude bring.

During the day, stop, quiet your mind, then, take 15 minutes at a time to reflect on a mantra of your choosing.

Affirmation: *I Live in the Now.*

Conscious living is a holistic way of life.
–Sharon Parris-Chambers

Living consciously is focused on this moment, breathing and allowing the breath to breathe you. "Conscious living" is not a buzz word used to replace the term "healthy lifestyle". For many the term is just nice sounding words. Not so with Conscious living. You may ask why? Conscious living is the highest form of healthy living, yet it goes a step further. It incorporates the spiritual with the physical, creating yoga, a union of mind body and spirit. It is the holistic approach to life, which takes in all aspects of our humanity. When we say conscious living, we tend to gravitate more towards the spiritual aspect. In this way we, will now consider this conscious and precious fleeting moment as all that we really have.

Sacred Practice: Guided Meditation.

Standing on your feet; close your eyes. Breathe in deeply, hold, exhale - long exhalations - emptying the lungs.

Do these three more times. "You are energy and vibration, the stuff that the universe is made of, in this very moment you are a particle of light, reflecting the grand universe. Why feel down and depressed? Take in the breath of life that express you, breathe you and resonate a feeling of oneness.

Take a moment now and suggest to your right hand that it is going to move on its own, away from your side, being raised by invisible threads like a puppet up to the sky. Let it down gently by reeling in the invisible threads, slow now, bring it down, down, down. Now feel the energy in the left hand being raised by an invisible energy puppet master. Raise it up, up gently, up to the sky. Then down, slowly, ever so slowly, feel every motion.

That was energy in motion. Did you enjoy that feeling? You can practice and repeat as often as you like. Go ahead and repeat that exercise again. Perhaps you can begin to investigate how energy can be used positively to enhance your life.

Here are some suggestions that may help you:

1. Use energy to focus your thoughts more, remove worry and fear.
2. Use energy to remove sickness from your body with the healing touch as practiced in Quantum Touch, Hands on Healing, Reiki and Pranic Healing.
3. Find quiet times to visualize the life you want to live now.

-Guided Meditation by Sharon Parris-Chambers

Affirmation: *I am energy and vibration.*

*Are you living life as a 'parentheses in
eternity' or are you really living?*
–Sharon Parris-Chambers

First of all, dear ones, we must recall how parentheses are used and their purpose. This grammatical construct is used to set things off for greater clarity or as an aside; an interlude or interval. As such, it is purposeful.

When we speak, we often do not say what we mean, so enter the parentheses, for greater clarity. When we say what we mean and mean what we say, there is no need to use the parentheses, outside of a mathematical equation.

Life is what it is, neither parentheses, comma nor exclamation point! It simply IS! When we dissect it, construct, re-construct and de-construct, we lose the meaning of life. Life is found in living and being. Two mystics exemplified this postulate in the following video. Deepak Chopra, author and doctor of Quantum Physics, and Sadhguru, founder of Isha Foundation, Mystic. In their discussion it was revealed that Sadhguru never participated in academic learning. His mind is clear and free, devoid of the preconditions of most people. Yet, he was still equal in awareness, and knowledge as his counterpart.

Dr Chopra, a medical doctor, studied all the Holy Scriptures and is fully immersed in science. In the end, these gurus meet on common ground. They walk a Spiritual path, moving from the Unknown to the Known, from the Un-manifest to Manifest. When you can distance yourself from Mind, which is a construct of human living, and be the Witness or Observer, you can experience what Sadhguru has for most of his life, i.e., freedom from thought expression. Sadhguru and Chopra have found "Nirvana" albeit through different paths. They are one with the universe, its expressions and its infinite manifestations of love and light. (Tandon, 2015)

Are you purposeful or are you empty? Are you open to Divine Spirit to move in and through your life to allow you to experience true freedom?

Sacred Practice:
Take 21 days for reflection, tranquility and some silence. Increase your meditative periods. Take quiet walks in the forest or park. Resist the impulse to have the last word. Enjoy the quiet interlude and freedom of resting the tongue, your two-edge sword.

Deep Breathing:
Spend more time breathing. Take deep breaths. When you inhale the stomach is pushed out like a balloon. The breathing apparatus in humans is the diaphragm. When you breathe out, observe the stomach contracting slowly in long breaths. It is the thoracic diaphragm that is doing most of the work. It is muscular, shaped like a dome, membranous and separates the thoracic (chest) and abdominal cavities in mammals. (Brittanica.com, 2013)

It is believed that "Shallow breathing is the root of all evil, but conscious deep breathing restores and secures our souls." (Desmond Green)

With shallow breathing, lungs, brain and cells become deficient in oxygen, which reduces our Divine nature to think and act intelligently. So, continue to breathe deeply every day. Practice deep breathing in the mornings on arising and at night before going to sleep.

Affirmation: *My breath is my beloved.*

Deny the Mist of the Mind with a
Positive Mental Attitude
–Sharon Parris-Chambers

You can deny the mist of the mind with positive thinking and a Positive Mental Attitude (PMA)!

Use a Mantra to access the positive forces, the angels in your higher consciousness, where your Temple of Inner Peace resides. When you feel your energy diminishing, check your breathing and thinking patterns. These can rob your energy and power.

You could feel down in the dumps or jaded anytime, but the key is what to do about it. You see, to live an active and joyous life, it is important to live in the moment. As you think and breathe, so are You. Are you a Shallow Breather or a Deep Breather? Whatever your answer, you can improve your breathing patterns and enjoy the joys of conscious living! Take deep breaths and make things happen, yes good things, by putting on your Positive Mental Attitude (PMA).

Quickly get back on track by removing the 'mist of the mind' with Conscious deep breathing, your Mantra and PMA.

Sacred Practice:
Daily practice deep breathing by taking rapid breaths through the nose like the panting of a dog. Count from the first to one hundred (100) breaths. If you feel dizzy, relax and start again. You will feel relaxed, refreshed and your lungs will be strengthened. Then enter the gap, that quiet space between thoughts. Relax into the meditation.

If negative thoughts arise, say "I will deal with this later" and keep focused on positivity. You are now on your way to removing the 'mist of the mind'.

Affirmation: *Only good things happen to me.*

My Dreams are not too big.
–Sharon Parris-Chambers

"Your dreams are not too big, weave them in your heart, speak them and live them." (Parris-Chambers, 2011)

When you live your life according to your personal vision of who you are and want to be, then you will realize the words spoken by Dr Wayne Dyer, one of the world's greatest motivators and spiritual teachers.

Dr Dyer once said, "The more you see yourself as what you'd like to become, and act as if what you want is already there, the more you'll activate those dormant forces that will collaborate to transform your dream into your reality."

I wrote the words "My dreams are not too big, I will weave them in my heart, speak them and live them" during a time of self-discovery and personal development. It was my attempt to push myself to my next level of achievement at a time when mediocrity was setting in. I was working, existing but reached a plateau. I wanted to achieve great things. So, I learned from spiritual thought leaders like Dr. Wayne Dyer, Les Brown, Theo Chambers, Og Mandino, Deepak Chopra, Iyanla Vanzant and Marianne Williamson. I began to picture myself as a winner, achieving great things and manifesting my destiny. The result is an amazing transformation which has changed my life.

Dyer always said: "See it when you believe it."

Theo Chambers, one of my most endearing mentors, has stressed for over thirty years, "You are the master of your destiny!"

Sacred Practice:
Daily find a quiet space to meditate, empty your mind. During this time, you can repeat your affirmation. In addition, you can visualize your dreams.

Take a deep breath, exhale, repeat until you are relaxed. Create a vision of your ideal self, focus on your body, your clothes and apparel.

You will focus on creating a positive mental attitude, see yourself in exotic and sacred places. Project into the future visioning your ideal home and environment and your ideal soul mate.

Remember: What you focus on expands into your reality. Spend quality time visioning the world of your creation. You are as you think.

Affirmation:
I AM *that* I AM.

Joy and Pain

The flip side of joy is pain. You can't have one without the other. This is the reality of the world of polarity that we live in. Just for a minute imagine a joyful world without pain or war. Oh, what a beautiful world it IS!

In the current paradigm we know Good vs. Bad, Happy vs. Sad, Black vs. White and Right vs. Might. Let us push the envelope together and create a joy-filled world of peace and love. See it, feel it, live it and become it.

See a beautiful world with beautiful people, fearing nothing and no one. People, organisms, plants and minerals are in harmony; there is no more war. Just peace, love and happiness. Aah! The joys of living without pain and suffering.

Let's take a page out of the book of the Bonobo monkeys. Let's make love, frolic and enjoy life as they do. They solve their problems with love and love making in their simplistic world. What can we learn from them?

We can use our divine imagination to create that world filled with the wonders and joys of living in a paradise earth. Go ahead! It is your vision, your movie. Create a world void of pain and suffering and filled with the joy of blissful living.

Sacred Practice: Find time daily to express love in the slightest to most profound passionate ways. It may be acknowledging someone with the words "I love and appreciate you." Or giving your smile to a stranger (It is free, go ahead!) or helping someone in need physically, emotionally and psychologically.

Sit quietly, breathing evenly; focus on your breath for one minute. Now, when relaxed. Imagine the world you want to live in: Peaceful, void of war, suffering or strife. Where people, organisms, minerals and plants are in harmony. There is no lack or limitation and Love is the only currency of exchange.

How do you feel about you and those around you? What are you willing to do to keep this lifestyle going? What transformational change has taken place in you? And what can you do to help others to experience this beautiful spiritual paradise while on earth?

Affirmation: *My divine joy brings no pain.*

The Presence is One in the Universe.
–Sharon Parris-Chambers

When you come from a sacred place, from a non-religious place or any space, you find one thing – *One Presence*. When you peel an onion, you find an open center that represent the infinite universe. When you peer into the human cell, you find a microcosm of the divine universe. The cell body consists of a nucleus, within the cytoplasm, there are organelles, the mitochondria, and other elements. These living entities are representative of human life, which replicates itself on demand. Each cell has the capacity to repair itself and to communicate with the other. Current estimates of the cells in the human body number 70-100 trillion. Yet, the important point is this, the body is one unit comprised of trillion of cells.

The universe is comprised of billions of orbital bodies having their own moon, sun and stars and they create new entities when they combust and coalesce. The presence in the universe that creates order, out of chaos, is also in us. We witness it every day. Now acknowledge the *Presence* within you.

Sacred Practice: **Chakra Meditation**.
Today you will learn to respect your own body system, honor each organ and express gratitude and love to each one in equanimity and honesty.

Play some relaxing music, preferably brainwave synchronization (find on Youtube.com). Choose one, then sit quietly, begin to breathe evenly from the diaphragm, in and out. When you are relaxed, visualize your body (standing). Visualize an aura around the body of golden or (white) light that extends out about one foot (1 meter). Bathe in the golden light for 15 minutes. Let it surround you as it emanates from the Crown Chakra. This is the Divine light. Then, gradually begin to visualize indigo (Royal Blue), the color of your third eye chakra also known as Ajna, (Sanskrit) which means to perceive, to command. It is the color that opens the consciousness and brings awareness to higher planes and connects us with the spiritual world. Visualize Turquoise light surrounding the Throat Chakra & minor chakra – find your voice, seek clarity in communication. Visualize Rose or Green light of the Heart chakra. Enjoy the warmth of rose consciousness, a feeling of empowerment, safety and security. Yellow light of the Solar plexus chakra. Yellow, reflective of the centre of our being; the color of sunshine. Feel the energy of the sun surround you now. The main energy of yellow is intellect. The Sacral Chakra, Orange color, is your passion and pleasure centre and it is in the pelvic area. It gives a sense of emotion, pleasure, connectedness, sensuality and intimacy. Vision orange light glowing all around you. Hold and then merge into the red dense color of the Root chakra.

The Sanskrit name is Muladhara, a combined term comprised of the words "root" and "support". Sit in a seated lotus position, visualize a red rose color surrounding the root chakra. Channel the color of this elemental energy of the first chakra down to the earth to ground you. If the root is out of alignment, then a range of imbalances throughout the body follow. Relax and enjoy the feeling of wellbeing.

It would be advisable to spend some time understanding the chakras, their meaning, as well as the physical and spiritual development associated with each one. This practice can be used as often as it is needed to balance your mind, body and spirit. For more information on the chakras, visit Chakra-Anatomy.com and Mindvalley.com

Affirmation: *I AM one with the Divine universe.*

Healing

Healing of the nation begins with me.
–Sharon Parris-Chambers

The healing of the nation which is central to healing the world begins with you. It is the same if you bring peace or love. Change must begin with 'me,' and every individual, one heart at a time. Beginning with this premise and understanding, is the first step to bringing the change you seek.

As a values facilitator, I assisted trainers in their use of Living Values Education since 2003 in Jamaica. The Values Education program is used in over 40 countries worldwide (www.livingvalues.net/jamaica). *The lessons began with Peace, followed by Love, Respect and the other values: freedom, cooperation, tolerance, happiness, honesty, humility, responsibility, simplicity and unity.*

The reason that we begin training with peace is that, peace is the essential physical state of human beings. Begin to heal yourself through daily meditation and reflection. Adding Affirmations to help you focus on changing your attitude and behaviors.

Develop a positive mental attitude (PMA). What is your attitude? It is what you are thinking and doing. Check it. Change wrong thinking before the thought manifests in your attitude by saying, 'Cancel, Cancel, Cancel' (three times). Cancel limiting thoughts from manifesting and begin to take control of your conscious thoughts. When you change your thoughts, you change your life. You will then be ready to tackle unconscious thoughts. Through the regular practice of visualization and meditation you can reduce and remove limiting beliefs.

Sacred Practice:

I have had success with the use of Dr. Shad Helmstetter's book, *What to Say When you Talk to Yourself*, which teaches how to recite positive affirmations with strong emotional impact leading to a replacement of negative cognitions with positive ones. This can be done by saying the affirmations and passages three (3) times. On the third time you would read it as though you were the Coach using the "you" form. This is most powerful, as the subconscious, is the place where real change occurs, the coach's voice has strong impact here. Below is a sample practice session. Go ahead give it a try.

Affirmations:

A sample of Shad Helmstetter's methodology:

1. "My balance and composure carry me through any situation. I have no need to be emotionally shallow. I am confident in the things I say and do."
2. "My balance and composure carry me through any situation. I have no need to be emotionally shallow. I am confident in the things I say and do."
3. "You are balanced and composed and follow through in any situation. You have no need to be emotionally shallow. You are confident in the things you say and do."

Healing of the nation begins with you healing each thought one-by-one. You must not give up, with persistence you will develop the strength, find your platform, and help create transformational world change.

My breath is my constitution for living.
—Sharon Parris-Chambers

Where would you be without your breath? Your breath is your constitution for living. It is your source that is animating you; breathing you. Feel the breath surging through you, giving you energy and vitality. When the breath or Chi (Ki) is blocked, then dis-ease sets in. It is important to keep the breath of life circulating freely and forcefully in your body.

When you stop breathing, are you anxious, frightened or angry? Oftentimes, we do not breathe evenly and rhythmically for a host of reasons, some of which are understandable. Now, let's be mindful of our breathing patterns and correct them.

Become more conscious of your breath that is breathing you. Enjoy the fullness of life, take deep breaths. Find the joy of living, find happiness through developing your relationship with the Divine universe, one breath at a time.

Sacred Practice: Try Reiki therapy and feel the energy flow through your entire body. Reiki can help balance your chakras (seven main energy vortexes within the spinal column that regulates body functions and emotions). Ask the therapist to direct the energy to any areas of pain in your body. Feel the response. While receiving Reiki, enjoy the Reiki/Zen music that is offered during the therapy and just relax into the flow of energy that is directed to your body. Accept it openly. Try Reiki again and other forms of energy therapies such as Pranic Healing, Quantum touch, Hands On healing and you will find one with which you resonate. Apply it regularly to balance your Chakras. Journal your experiences.

Affirmation: *I AM one with my breath which breathes me.*

Life

Imagine the life you want to live and
then live it one moment at a time.
—Sharon Parris-Chambers

Go ahead, create your own movie, the image of your life, the life you want to live every moment. Yes, see it so clear in your mind's eye so that you can reach out and touch it.

You can begin right now, do not wait. You have waited long enough.

A quote comes to mind from the *Sage Within*, a book written by Theo Chambers, about the first female sage who lived in the village of Watanama, twenty-five thousand feet above sea level. Goddess Farinah was honored with the name, The Anointed One because she dared to live her dream to become a sage in a village where only men were groomed to be sages. Upon being appointed and initiated the Grand Master of the Mystical Order of The Sages, The Anointed One declared "many Sages have argued that women had never been and could never be ordained since they were physically, mentally and spiritually inferior to men. Today, I call for the awakening of the Sage that is sleeping inside of every woman to rise and claim their rightful position as equal to all male on planet earth." (Chambers, 2014)

Today, imagine the life you want to live and then live it one moment at a time. It is the same journey of the Anointed One in the fictional story. Rise to the occasion and allow your soul's calling to stir within you and to manifest your destiny.

Sacred Practice:

Close your eyes, take a deep breath, exhale. Do this until you are feeling relaxed. Now, picture yourself happy, feeling joyful for no reason just to know that you are alive. See yourself in a field of lilies or lavender. Smell the radiant and relaxing fragrance. See the vibrant colors: yellow, white, orange, peach, purple, pink and lavender. Feel the breeze blowing on your skin. Look ahead, notice the mineral spring nearby just below the hillside where you are. Walk towards it. You are going downhill, one tier at a time. At each tier, you see a different vista. The mist of the mountains. The sunny skies below the clouds; the cool shade under the grove of trees. You are two tiers above the mineral spring. Down, you go; you see the butterflies and birds and their beautiful patterns & colors. Further down, you touch the soil of the banks and step into the cool water. There you sit and soak up the minerals; rejuvenating and healing your mind, body and soul.

- Guided Meditation by Sharon Parris-Chambers

Now, as you relax, ask yourself these questions: What do I want most in life? What will I enjoy doing, even if I were not paid to do it?

I suggest these questions because, you may lose the things of the world, but you would have gained something far more everlasting.

The joy, the happiness of being in a world that you create; peace, love and shared values is more meaningful than acquiring things.

You will ask Divine Spirit (God) to guide you and to open your consciousness to know your purpose. Stay alert, awake and you will be guided to your greatest good. The key is to trust in the universe and not to depend on your egotistic mind to provide the answers. If you do that, ego will lead you astray. Strengthen your defenses and become grounded in your own spiritual development now. Namastè

Affirmation: *The beautiful life I envision has now manifested.*

Lifestyle Transformation

*I AM life's expression of the Divine universe.
I AM manifesting as a Divine being and
my light has transformative powers.*
—Sharon Parris-Chambers

In my search for truth this is what I always wanted to achieve: Becoming a Divine being and letting my light shine. What about you?

When you live the life of a Divine being manifesting your destiny with each breath, what you think, you manifest. You become responsible for every thought.

With each stage of your spiritual development, through your reflection (meditation) you are strengthened. You begin this journey in obedience to the will of the Divine. You will realize your dharma, purpose in life, and your light will continue to shine as a beacon unto others.

Practice:
Read the "Passion Test" (The Effortless path to Discovering Your Life Purpose) by Janet Bray Attwood and Chris Attwood. Learn to identity your Passion, your inner drive to achieve your unique gift or talent. Read Janet's unique story. Let it motivate you. Then, take the Passion Test. Go to www.ThePassionTest.com. Do the work and you will begin to see real positive change manifest in your life.

Passion Test Program:

- ☐ Write your top five (5) passions and review often.
- ☐ Apply this Mantra to life's challenges: Attention, Intention, No Tension.
  When you focus on your passion there is no tension. Go on the path of least tension. When you do, your Passion should always come first.
- ☐ Creating Markers for your success so you know when you get there.
- ☐ Focus on what you want or something better. Never underestimate yourself. (Atwood, 2008)

Affirmation: *"I intend to feel successful and attract prosperity."* (Wayne Dyer)

Appendix

Meditative Sacred Practices

(These sacred practices are similar to the
ones in the previous chapters.)

1. **Quiet Sitting**.
   Sacred Practice: Sit in quiet reflection observing your breath
   for 15 minutes. Perform the asanas in the Sun Salutation. End
   with open arms above your head, claiming our abundance and
   giving thanks for that which is coming into your life. Return to
   15 minutes of reflection.

   Write your experiences in your journal.

   Affirmation: *I am open and receptive to the Divine universe.*

2. **Quiet Reflection**.
   Sit in quiet reflection. Focus on our breath. Begin now for 15 to
   30 minutes. Inhale and exhale. Relax. Choose a short phrase or
   mantra to direct your thoughts. E.g. ***I AM that I AM.***

   Modern day mantras:
   "This too shall pass." (Endurance/Strength)
   "I change my thoughts, I change my world." (Norman Vincent
   Peale)

"I love you, I'm sorry, Please forgive me and Thank you."
(Hawaiian Prayer of Forgiveness, Ho'oponopono)
"Every day in every way I'm getting better and better."(Laura Silva)

Some favorite ancient mantras:
"Aum"|"Om" (Sanskrit/Hindu – means "It is")
"I AM that I AM" (Hebrew, "Ayer Asher Ayah" - God's name)
"Om Namah Shivaya"(Hindu, I honor the divinity within myself)
"Om Mani Padme Hum" (Hail the Buddha, Jewel in the Lotus.)

3. **Let Go.**

   Your thoughts can become aimless and restless when you sit in meditation. Use the mantra to guide your thoughts, keeping the flow positive. Breathe deeply; inhale and exhale, take 10 deep breaths. Continue breathing. Your breath might become shallow. During this time, you may be reflecting on a troublesome thought or idea. Let it go, relax, breathe deeply and follow the breath.

   Do not give in. Your breath is your guide during these explorations. Meditation is no mystery. It really is a state of mind, not an activity.

   Affirmation: *In Divine Consciousness, I live, move and have my being.*

4. **Bless Humanity with Peace & Love.**

   You enter meditation as a conscious activity. When we practice the rudiments of accessing the spirit realm, that is our original home, it becomes easy to go in and out of consciousness at will. You are now learning how to master your destiny. Your awareness level will increase, you will use access to Spirit for positive and healing purposes. We will not deal with the dark side of spiritual power. Our purpose is to bless and heal humanity with Peace and Love.

Affirmation: *I AM blessed as I bless others.*

5. **Extinguish Ego Distractions**.
Sit in a quiet place, clear your mind of distractions. Begin to breathe, taking long inhalations and then long exhalations. When you begin to feel relaxed, create in your mind's eye a picture of happiness, joy and laughter. Recall moments in time that took your breath away. Saturate your mind with these pleasant images. Just be in this moment.

Ego distractions always appear when you sit for meditation. Just be in this moment. Create your intentions for the day, ask your questions, such as: "What is my purpose in life?" "What am I to do and how am I to do it?" Continue to sit in meditation and the answers will come, if not then, later. But they will.

Write down the thoughts and answers to your questions. Do this every day and night to develop the pattern of listening to your Higher Self, your Divine Self.

Affirmation: *My presence is a Divine Gift.*

6. **Heart of A Rose**.
Another effective practice is looking into the heart of a freshly cut Rose. Find a quiet place in nature or in the quiet of your room. Begin to stare at the center of the Rose, its heart. A Rose is much like life: you will meet thorns along the way, but if you have faith and believe in your dreams you will eventually move beyond the thorns into the essence of the flower. Keep staring at the rose. Notice its color, texture and design. Savor its fragrances and think only about this thing of beauty in front of you.

At first, other thoughts will enter your mind, gently say, "I will deal with these later." Simply return your attention to the object of your focus. Soon your mind will grow strong and disciplined. Excerpt - "The Heart of the Rose" from <u>The Monk who sold his Ferrari</u> by Robin Sharma.

When you practice seeing the beauty in you and humanity, you will begin to develop a spiritual consciousness and a disciplined mind that will lead to the desires of your heart, to living your passion and dreams. Practice this exercise regularly and manifest your destiny.

Affirmation: *I see the beauty in me and humanity.*

7. **Go to the Mirror**.
On awakening, go to the mirror. Love the person that you see in the mirror every day. Look at your reflection. Say to that person staring at you, I LOVE YOU, MWAH (Kiss your reflection.) When you can do this without criticism. You are ready to face the world!

Do this every day for 30 days to reinforce Self-Esteem & Self-Confidence.

Affirmation: *I am Beauty Personified.*

Mirror Work:
Practice looking in the Mirror daily and go within, to the mirror of your being, and say: "I love you." You will begin to heal the child within with these words. Do this every day for as long as you need to. Sometimes, say "You are the best!", "You are Great!". The mirror exercise is very effective in honoring your greatness.

Affirmation: *I enjoy being me.*

Mirror Image.
Stand in front of the mirror and speak to your mirror image. Cross your hands over your heart and gaze into your eyes. Say: "I love me and I honor me." "I will never allow anyone to hurt or abuse me." "I will never give up on me." "I love my life and enjoy being alive."

Then turn it around as if you are the Coach speaking and say: "I love you and I honor you." "I will never allow anyone to hurt or abuse you." I will never give up on you." Love the life you live and enjoy yourself."

Smile and visualize the feeling of being loved by your parents, friends and family. Enjoy these vibrations. Repeat as often as necessary. Write your experiences in your journal.

Affirmation: *I love me and I honor me.*

8. **Source of Creation**.
Breathe deeply, exhale and relax. Enter meditation. Your only focus is: *"I am the Source of Creation not a piece of creation. I command my mind, body and spirit to raise my conscious awareness of who I am. I reach out to my Ankhsestors and connect with each one..."* Call their names. After calling their names, continue to breathe deeply and focus on the Mantra. Write down all thoughts and ideas that arise.

Offering to Ankhsestors (Ancestors). This is an additional step for those who perform Rituals. Go to the ocean or water source. Open with prayer, then make an offering to Oshun (mother of sweet waters or fresh water) or in her form as mother of salt water (Yemanja). Take coffee beans grounded, rice (signifying abundance), milk (generativity), salt (protection) and offer to Oshun/Yemanja. Ask for what you want, give thanks and close with prayer.

Affirmation: *I AM a Creator not a piece of creation.*

9. **Divine Healing Breaths**.
Sit in meditation daily for 15 to 30 minutes. Inhale and exhale, relax. Choose a short phrase or mantra ("I am a clear channel for Divine good") to direct your thoughts. Keeping the breath even:

1) Breathe in and hold for count of 12.
2) Exhale for count of 12 Repeat cycle 10 times.
3) Relax

Journal your experiences.

Affirmation: *I am a Potent Powerhouse of Potentiality; I can access Divine Spirit with each breath.*

10. **Law of Least Effort**.
I practice daily the Law of Least Effort by visualizing what I want in life. I go into a quiet zone and visualize what I wish to manifest. Doing this regularly, creates a shift from the unmanifest (unconscious) to manifest (conscious) states.

Affirmation: *I am guided every day to make right choices.*

11. **Guided Meditation**.
Standing on your feet; close your eyes. Breathe in deeply, hold, exhale - long exhalations - emptying the lungs.

Do these three more times. "You are energy and vibration, the stuff that the universe is made of, in this very moment you are a particle of light, reflecting the grand universe. Why feel down and depressed? Take in the breath of life that express you, breathe you and resonate a feeling of oneness.

Take a moment now and suggest to your right hand that it is going to move on its own, away from your side, being raised by invisible threads like a puppet up to the sky. Let it down gently by reeling in the invisible threads, slow now, bring it down, down, down. Now feel the energy in the left hand being raised by an invisible energy puppet master. Raise it up, up gently, up to the sky. Then down, slowly, ever so slowly, feel every motion.

That was energy in motion. Did you enjoy that feeling? You can practice and repeat as often as you like. Go ahead and repeat that exercise again. Perhaps you can begin to investigate how energy can be used positively to enhance your life.

Here are some suggestions that may help you:

1. Use energy to focus your thoughts more, remove worry and fear.
2. Use energy to remove sickness from your body with the healing touch as practiced in Quantum Touch, Hands on Healing, Reiki and Pranic Healing.
3. Find quiet times to visualize the life you want to live now.

-Guided Meditation by Sharon Parris-Chambers

Affirmation: *I am energy and vibration.*

12. **Contemplate a Koan**.
Note: Koans are an ancient tradition of stories, phrases, poems or statements that were identified, though the years, for their transformational ability. Sometimes a koan is a recounting of the circumstances that lead to the awakening of a student. Sometimes they shock. Sometimes they confuse, but always, the koan interacts with something deeper than the mind.

A koan may appear non-nonsensical, but a koan is not a riddle or a puzzle. It cannot be solved by understanding it. Only when it reveals something new about your true nature, when something in you shifts in response, will you become intimate with the koan.

Sitting in Zazen, assuming the lotus posture, enter meditation. Choose a koan to contemplate.

A) When the many are reduced to one, to what is the one reduced?
B) When you can do nothing, what can you do?
C) What is your original face before you were born?

Source: (TheBuddahfultao.com, 2012)

13. Sit in a quiet place. Take some deep breaths. Repeat again until you are relaxed. You are in a state of spiritual awareness in tune with your Divine self. Continue taking deep breaths. Explore the thoughts of "who am I?" Write reflections in your journal.

    Think of yourself as you truly are, as Consciousness, Energy and Vibration. The Force that is breathing you. Remove the thoughts of me, myself, mother, brother, sister, husband and wife, right now. You are Consciousness. Moving and flowing in creation. You can take any form. You are boundless and you create effortlessly through your thoughts and imagination. You can always come to this place to restore, re-create, rejuvenate, revivify and resurrect your spirit. You are never wanting there. The vibration of love and light abounds. Hold this conscious intention now, and throughout the day. Return here any time you need inspiration and rejuvenation.

14. **Quiet Contemplation**.
    Sit in meditation allowing no thought interference for 15-30 minutes. Remain calm and quiet inside, open to the sensory and vibratory sensations of your body, amid the sensations maintain your composure. Write your experiences in your journal.

15. **Enter the Gap**.
    Enter meditation, breathe deeply, relax and affirm your Divine Good. For example, intone: "*Today, I extend One Love to all Humanity.*"

    Take a minimum of 5 -15 minutes and relax into your breath. Breathe in – Brief Hold – Breathe Out. Repeat. Again. You will receive benefits in mind, body and spirit as you continue to sit in meditation.

Say "This is my quiet time, I will deal with all emergencies later." Allow your breath to breathe you, becoming relaxed. Enter the Gap, being fully conscious and aware.

Affirmation: *I AM a peaceful soul.*

16. **Peace Be Unto You**.
    Retreat to your Temple of Inner Peace, go inward to your inner sanctuary. Focus on your breath; use breathing exercises to move the breath and allow these words to transport you to higher consciousness: There is quiet there, an ocean of peace and tranquility permeates your consciousness. You are one with it. There is no separation. You escape your troubles in body and mind. You are pure energy and vibration. You think thoughts and they manifest in physical form. You emanate light; You are transformed into your subtle body. You are light, your original source.

    Stay in this consciousness until you are ready to return to the now.

    Affirm your Divine good by saying: *"I am a Divine being, a point of light and reflection of the Divine Universe."*

    Repeat the Peace Mantra: *"I AM Peace Flowing unbounded in the universe."* Repeat for as long as you desire. **Record your experience of this practice.**

17. **Follow Your Breath**.
    Take the next 30 minutes to relax your body by taking some deep breaths. Go deep within. Follow your breath. Take strong even breaths, relax after each one. Welcome the godhead or goddess of your being and say you are ready to explore the spiritual you. Allow your inner vision to take over your physical faculties and explore the hidden you. Ask questions and listen for the answers which will arise in you as a palpable feeling, a

voice, image or impression. Make a point to remember to write in your journal when you return from your adventure.

Affirmation: *I and my breath are one.*

18. **Unify the World Around One Love**
Sit in meditation, begin to focus on your breath. Relax fully. Begin to visualize the earth as a small ball in your open hands. Send blessings of love and light to the earth. Reach deep within to access your Divine love and send it from your I AM Presence to the I AM presence of each person on earth through the ball. Focus your intention on the small ball in your hand, which is a symbol of earth. Continue for 15 minutes or more read or recite an inspirational Psalm, Poetry or Mantra of your choice to close your meditative practice.

You may do this exercise any time you wish to share love and light with your family, friends or humanity.

Affirmation: *I AM Love and Light*

19. **Sacred Practice**: Mindfulness Meditation.
Mindfulness meditation also known as Vipassana and insight meditation, requires focus on mindfulness practice. Awareness of the object of meditation, the breath, sounds, or all the above.

HOW:

1. Assume a comfortable but alert upright position.
2. Gently bring your attention to the breath and note each inhalation and exhalation – without trying to change anything or breathe in any specific way.
3. When you notice your mind wandering (as it often does) gently bring your attention back to the breath and start again. At this point, you can choose to focus on a Mantra.

Continue your mindfulness meditation for as long as you wish.

Affirmation: *"Spirit have your way in my life."*

20. **Self-control.**
    For one month, I will practice self-control in words, thoughts and action. I will write my daily observations in my diary and learn from them.

    Affirmation: *I speak, think and act with humility and self-control.*

21. **Become Love.**
    When you become love, forgiving others is automatic; it is a snap. Start by forgiving yourself first. Forgive the biggest mistake you have made in your life. Then forgive the smallest mistake. When you are comfortable being free of guilt, turn your attention to forgiving others.

    Picture yourself seated across from someone who has done you wrong and speak your words of forgiveness to them. End with a prayer and this **Affirmation**: *Love forgives all.*

22. **Visualization before Manifestation.**
    Sit in a comfortable position, inhale cleansing breaths, exhale forcefully stale air. Repeat a few times. Now, close your eyes and visualize (picture) yourself as the person that you want to be, loved and respected. Go ahead and live your life from the inside out. See your success through visualization before manifestation. Record your visualization(s) in your diary.

    Affirmation: *I accept my power to visualize my reality.*

23. **Twin Hearts Meditation.** Go to Youtube.com and search for: Twin Hearts Meditation by Master Choa Kok Sui, founder of Pranic Healing or his senior student Master Stephen Co. and watch video *The Twin Hearts Meditation* teaches how to bring heart and crown chakra in alignment. Experience the exhilaration of divine healing. Use the "Om" mantra. In between "Oms" please concentrate on the Silence. When

practiced regularly with focus and concentration, you can reach an awakened state of awareness.

Affirmation: *I have the power to heal my life*

24. **See it, Feel it and Become it**.
Sit quietly, breathing deeply; inhale and exhale. Repeat until you are very relaxed. See yourself surrounded by the power and transparence of golden light. Now, become the Light. It is your original source. Imagine the sun, the stars, and their energies. Earth reflects the universe of which it is a part. The stars collide to create new universes, and, *as without so within*, we too are part of this phenomenon.

We are starlight. See it, believe it and become it. Remain in this form for as long as you can.

Next, see yourself as love (see the color Rose reflective of the Heart Chakra, the seat of love and intuition.) Feel a vibration of warm energy surging through your being. I am speaking of Divine love, or universal love, that encompasses humanity as One Heart and One Self. Yes, One Love. This love is not dependent on anyone or anything; it is the fullness and the totality of all there is. Open your heart center to this energy. See it, Feel it and Become it. Practice this every day and soon you will be filled with Light and Love, transforming and transcending from your physical essence into a spiritual one. Now, share your Divine Love with every being on the planet, one heart at a time.

Affirmation: *Divine intelligence is a vibration within me and I am one with it.*

25. **Breath of Fire & Five Tibetan Rites of Rejuvenation**.
Sitting comfortably with your back straight. Begin to do the 'Breath of Fire' exercise. It is rapid breathing like a dog panting. Do these 100 times, forcibly. How do you feel? If there is

144

discomfort, stop and relax. As you continue to do this exercise, you will strengthen your lungs enabling it to take in more air. Now, continue with your activities or rest and enjoy this feeling of wellbeing and freedom.

Thereafter breathe naturally and deeply from the diaphragm.

Listen to the 'Five Tibetan Rites of Rejuvenation' CD on YouTube and begin to learn how to strengthen your core and protect against disease. Research shows that Monks have used these rites to increase their vitality and longevity.

My dear friend, a writer and yogini, Rachel Citrin is over 90 years of age. She is alert, flexible and practices these sacred rites daily. Rachel says it is important to "keep moving." She taught me the "Five Tibetan Rites of Rejuvenation" exercise in Jamaica as part of a writing workshop, which was combined with breathing exercises and prayer, in preparation to communicate with the Muse or Sage within. Since then, I have taught over 15 persons the Tibetan Rites of Rejuvenation. Rachel uses the positive energy and flexibility from the Tibetan Rites to fuel her movement in Danza de Alma classes in Mexico or where ever in the world she travels. Journal your experiences.

Affirmation: I AM Love and Life (Repeat Often)

26. **Law of Least Effort**.
    Practice daily the Law of Least Effort by visualizing what I want to enter my life for a minimum of 30 minutes in the morning and in the evening. The Law of Least Effort says:

A. *I will practice Acceptance. Today I will accept people, situations, circumstances, and events as they occur. I will know that this moment is as it should be, because the whole universe is as it should be. I will not struggle against the whole universe by struggling against this moment. My acceptance is total and complete. I accept things as they are this moment, not as I wish they were.*

B. *Having accepted things as they are, I will take Responsibility for my situation and for all those events I see as problems. I know that taking responsibility means not blaming anyone or anything for my situation (and this includes myself). I also know that every problem is an opportunity in disguise, and this alertness to opportunities allows me to take this moment and transform it into a greater benefit.*

C. *Today my awareness will remain established in Defenselessness. I will relinquish the Need to defend my point of view, and I will feel no need to persuade others to accept my point of view. I will remain open to all points of view and not be rigidly attached to any one of them.* (Chopra, 2018)

I go into a quiet zone and visualize what I wish to manifest. Doing this regularly creates a shift from the unconscious to conscious states. Practice the Law of Least Effort often; through its application you will transform into your Divine Self.

Affirmation: *I am a microcosm of the universe.*

27. **I AM Peace**.
Affirm your Divine good with these words: "*I am a Being of Peace and Love. I reflect that which I AM, not my marginalized self. I AM a Divine being, a point of light and reflection of the Divine Universe.*"

Repeat the Peace Mantra: "*I AM Peace Flowing unbounded in the universe.*"
Record your experience of repeating your Peace Mantra for 10 minutes.

28. **Self-Control**.

For one month I will practice self-control in words, thoughts and action. I will write my daily observations in my diary and learn from them.

Affirmation: *I speak, think and act in humility and self-control.*

29. **Self-Talk Session**.

I have had success with the use of Dr Shad Helmstetter's book, *What to Say When You Talk to Yourself*. This book was loaned to Theo and me by our doctor Tony Vendryes; it has been an invaluable Self-Help tool. It teaches the reader to recite positive affirmations with strong emotional impact, over time, negative cognitions are replaced with positive ones. This can be done by saying the affirmations and passages 3 times. On the third time you read it as though you were the Coach using the "you" form. This is most powerful, as the subconscious is the place where real change occurs. The coach voice has strong impact here. Below is a sample practice session.

Affirmations: Sample Shad Helmstetter approach:

1. *"My balance and composure carry me through any situation. I have no need to be emotionally shallow. I am confident in the things I say and do."*

2. *"My balance and composure carry me through any situation. I have no need to be emotionally shallow. I am confident in the things I say and do.*

3. *"You are balanced and composed and follow through in any situation. You have no need to be emotionally shallow. You are confident in the things you say and do."*

Healing of the nation begins with you healing each thought one by one. You must not give up, with persistence you will develop the strength, find your voice, and help create transformational world change.

30. **Visualization - Joy**.
Create a space where you are free from worry and daily concerns. Relax and enjoy the feeling of weightlessness, freedom and happiness. Now, take a few deep breaths. Visualize yourself in your favorite place of relaxation, such as a meadow, river or garden. See yourself happy, carefree and enjoying each moment of the day. Visualize yourself in this scenario and internalize these words:

> *"I am happy and carefree, enjoying this moment in time by the river. The water is clear and cool on this hot summer day. I feel like jumping in, but I will start by putting my feet in first. Aaah, that feels nice, its heavenly!" Sitting down, I promise myself that I will take time out to enjoy this moment at the river bank. A flock of gray and white birds fly overhead, making some 'squawky' sounds. They line up in a wondrous V formation. I look up at the azure blue sky and smile. Being in nature is having a positive and calming effect on me.*

> *I see a set of steps leading to the beach. I rise and begin to follow the path which is lined by beautiful ginger red flowers, birds of paradise sunset red and orange hanging flowers, and thumburgia purple delicate flowers on a meandering vine. And there are various species of ferns and orchids. I descend, while savoring every moment. I smile and tell myself that I am so fortunate to be enjoying this quiet moment in time. I approach the bottom. I looked around and saw the same kind of lush colorful beauty around me. I arrive at sea level and immediately ran to the pink sand beach and jump into the coolest, most refreshing water! I swam for what seemed like 20 minutes.*

I enjoy the moment, returning to my place of rest. It is there I saw a few persons walking towards me while I frolic in the water. A man and woman walk up and says "hello". I replied "hello, how are you?" The woman said, "enjoying the beauty of this perfect day." "Have you seen any starfish, stingray or jellyfish today?" "Yes, I have seen some starfish, but luckily no jellyfish today." Like me, they sat and stared out to sea. Soon, I felt the urge to begin walking back alone, so that I could enjoy the beautiful landscape, flora and fauna. "I will be leaving now, it was a pleasure meeting you both," I said, and slowly walked away.

-Guided Meditation by Sharon Parris-Chambers.

Repeat the above in the 'third person' as though are the Coach. This approach will have a profound impact by rewriting negative feelings with positive ones in your subconscious mind. Begin with the following: *"You are happy and carefree, enjoying this moment in time down by the river... Repeat the above scenario.*

I return to this conscious now moment, refreshed and rejuvenated. I smile easily and know that my joy is in each conscious moment spent being aware of nature around me, paying attention to people, places and things. I know intuitively that everything will work out in the fullness of time. If you must force something to happen, perhaps it won't happen. Instead, just step back and allow the Universe to help you or orchestrate the desired outcome.

Affirmation: *I remove the mist of my mind and find joy.*

31. **Traffic Control of the Mind.**
    Every hour on the hour, engage in traffic control of the mind. Sit in a quiet place. Resolve that nothing will keep you from quieting your mind for the next 5 minutes. Stop thinking and focus on a mantra. Such as: "I AM that I AM", "Peace Be still"

or "I am Love and Light." Do this for 5 minutes. Resume what you were doing previously.

You may also choose times to retreat to your Inner Temple based on your schedule. Note, though, that the ancients have long said that the period before sunrise is most fortuitous for contemplation and mediation.

Quiet the mind, focus on your Mantra, a Candle or, your Breath. Relax and then Record your experience.

This practice, when applied regularly will help you to focus your thoughts and actions, enabling you to become the master of your destiny.

Affirmation: *I live In the Now moment of eternity.*

32. **Breathdancing ™ with Prana Energy.**
    Breathe deeply now, take in the breath of life. You are breathdancing ™ using Prana energy. Inhale and Exhale. Relax and follow the breath…Follow the breath. You are going on a journey to discover the inner you. This is a place where you sometimes forget to visit. You are going there now, to your Temple of Inner Peace. Using your thoughts, feelings, sensory perceptions visualize yourself inside the place called YOU.

    Turn your intention to your inner Self. In this place called YOU, you can be yourself. There is no one to criticize or hurt you. Relax and say with meaning: *"I love me, I love every part of my body. I have nothing to fear. I am a Divine being filled with love, light, energy and vibration."*

    Breathe deeply now, take in the breath of life. You are breathdancing ™ using Prana energy. Inhale and exhale. Relax and follow the breath.

Affirmation: *I am breathing and morphing into the conscious awareness of One Self.*

33. **I AM My Breath**.
When you have reinforced your sacred life, you would have entered a paradise previously unknown.

Choose the right time to mediate. Schedule the most opportune times and location. Consistency facilitates the meditative depth you seek.

Take deep cleansing breaths. Deep breaths that brings in the Life Energy. Use that life energy to create your world, **not of fear**, but positivity, success and prosperity.

Sit in Zazen, quiet contemplative meditation. Use a mantra of your choice. You determine how long to sit based on your intuition. Write your experience in your journal.

Affirmation: *My breath is my beloved.*

34. **Lose Yourself in Nature**.
Take 15 to 30 minutes daily for 30 days and lose yourself in nature. Vacate your conscious mind and find your true ego-less self. If at first you cannot empty the mind, persist by walking in nature and being enthralled by the things around you. Refrain from judgment. Just be. Write your reflections in your journal each day. At the end of the 30 days read the entire month's activity and see how much you have grown spiritually.

Affirmation: *I AM all that.*

35. **Water and I are One**.
Go to the ocean or river today. Immerse yourself in water, relax and be one with it. Become water. Fluid, buoyant and unbounded.

Nature's water source is best. Just focus on the present moment. Watch the ebb and flow of nature before you.

Take note of the energy and vibration of water and be like water. It is you and you are water; it comprises 70% of your body. Take note of how you feel during and after immersion. Write your observations in your journal. This is your journey, make the best of it.

Affirmation: *I AM water and nothing stops my flow.*

36. **Unify Mind, Body & Spirit.**
    Divine Spirit of my higher Self, rid me of ego and a sense of separation. Merge me with you, who are my own Self. And so it is. -Mooji

    Affirmation: *I am my transcendent Self*

37. **Universal Oneness.**
    Begin and end the day totally in alignment with the universe. Let every thought that fire into your consciousness and every Divine action be in harmony with Peace and Love. Do this upon awaking, enter meditation, using the sound of creation "AAH (as in Hallelujah) in your sacred place for a minimum of 15 minutes. During the day, actively monitor your thoughts, and in the evening, begin meditation using the "OHM" sound of creation for 15 minutes. Then, relax into your being as a peaceful soul. In this state of spiritual wellness, the whole being experiences relaxation.

    Affirmation: *I AM one with the universe.*

38. **Let Life Touch You.**
    Sit quietly today during daybreak and again at sunrise. Relax, deep inhale, deep exhale; Relax. Repeat. Light a candle and watch its flame; this is to teach you to focus your attention. While looking at the candle, begin to focus on your quiet

rhythmic breathing; Relax. Allow your thoughts to come and go. Do not focus on them. This is your quiet time to empty the mind of its worries, fears and anxieties. After a while, you will begin to feel light, empty and joyful.

Do this every day for 30 days and journal your experiences.

Affirmation: *I love the life I live and I live the life I love.*

39. **Cleansing Breaths.**
Basic Pranayama – Alternative Nasal Breathing

Sit comfortably with spine erect and hips relaxed. Eyes closed. Inhale, close the right nostril with the thumb and breathe out through the left nostril. Breathe in through the left nostril and then with the ring finger close right nostril. Release the thumb on the right nostril and breathe out through the right nostril. Inhale through the right nostril, close with the thumb, release the ring or index finger from the left side and exhale through the left nostril.

These two full breaths represent one round of Alternate Nostril Breath. Do five to nine rounds. You should always inhale through the same nostril you just exhaled through. (Ashby, G., QiSynthesis: Journey to a Greater You in 30 days, 2018.)

Affirmation: *My breath is my constitution for living.*

40. Inhale-Focus-Connect.
Use this simple practice to Connect to Chi energy:
Inhale – Focus – Connect – Ask your question.
Exhale - Focus – Connect
Inhale – Focus – Connect – Ask your question.
Exhale – Focus - Connect
Repeat for ten rounds and relax. You may choose to stay with the first question or ask new questions.

Just Shift your attention from negativity to a positive mental attitude.

Focus your mind and connect to the universe.
Do it every time and be blessed with new energy.
Look ahead and feel the surge
Be free from stress; Create new synergy.
Just Shift – Focus and Connect to the universe.

Inhale – Focus – Connect – Ask your question.
Exhale - Focus – Connect
Inhale – Focus – Connect – Ask your question.
Exhale – Focus - Connect
Just Shift your attention away from worry and fear, connect to Divine consciousness.

Focus your mind and connect to the universe.
Wake up to a new reality of universal oneness.
When you Shift – Focus and Connect to the universe.

Affirmation: *I experience life as it is.*

41. **Sacred Practice:** Sit in a quiet place, begin to settle yourself. If questions arise in your mind, say "I will deal with these later." Take a deep breath, hold, exhale. Repeat as often as you need until you are relaxed. Now, begin to follow your breath until you are one with it. Introduce your question(s) and allow the answers to come forward as impulses or clear responses within your being. Listen to that quiet voice or the loud response that you have been waiting for. Accept these spiritual gifts and give thanks silently. Continue to ask other questions, or just relax into your being as energy and vibration.

   Affirmation: *I AM a being of limitless potentiality.*

42. **Write your Gratitude List**

Upon awakening daily, write down at least 10 things that you are grateful for. At the end of the week review all entries and enjoy the feeling of great joy, fulfillment and prosperity that humility and gratitude bring.

During the day, stop, quiet your mind, then, take 15 minutes at a time to reflect on a mantra of your choosing.

Affirmation: *I Live in the Now*

43. **Chakra Meditation.**

Today you will learn to respect your own body system, honor each organ and express gratitude and love to each one in equanimity and honesty.

Play some relaxing music, preferably brainwave synchronization (find on Youtube.com). Choose one, then sit quietly, begin to breathe evenly from the diaphragm, in and out. When you are relaxed, visualize your body (standing). Visualize an aura around the body of golden or (white) light that extends out about one foot (1 meter). Bathe in the golden light for 15 minutes. Let it surround you as it emanates from the Crown Chakra. This is the Divine light. Then, gradually begin to visualize indigo (Royal Blue), the color of your third eye chakra also known as Ajna, (Sanskrit) which means to perceive, to command. It is the color that opens the consciousness and brings awareness to higher planes and connects us with the spiritual world. Visualize Turquoise light surrounding the Throat Chakra & minor chakra – find your voice, seek clarity in communication. Visualize Rose or Green light of the Heart chakra. Enjoy the warmth of rose consciousness, a feeling of empowerment, safety and security. Yellow light of the Solar plexus chakra. Yellow, reflective of the centre of our being; the color of sunshine. Feel the energy of the sun surround you now. The main energy of yellow is intellect. The Sacral Chakra, Orange color, is your passion and pleasure centre and it is in the pelvic area. It gives a sense of emotion, pleasure, connectedness, sensuality and intimacy. Vision orange light glowing all around you. Hold and then merge into the red dense color of the Root chakra.

The Sanskrit name is Muladhara, a combined term comprised of the words "root" and "support". Sit in a seated lotus position, visualize a red rose color surrounding the root chakra. Channel the color of this elemental energy of the first chakra down to the earth to ground you. If the root is out of alignment, then a range of imbalances throughout the body follow. Relax and enjoy the feeling of wellbeing.

It would be advisable to spend some time understanding the chakras, their meaning, as well as the physical and spiritual development associated with each one. This practice can be used as often as it is needed to balance your mind, body and spirit. For more information on the chakras, visit Chakra-Anatomy.com and MindValley.com.

Affirmation: *I AM one with the Divine universe.*

Works Cited

Alaji, A., Heraldess. Affirmations. www.Adamaspeaks.com

Alpha, R. Gateway Radio Podcast Creator/CEO at Gateway2thegods. com https://gateway2thegods.com/2014/09/20/42

Ashby, G. (2016). *Anam Cara: Your Soul Friend and Bridge to Enlightenment and Creativity.* New York: Ashby, Glenville, Dr.

Ashby, G., QiSynthesis Journey to a Greater You in 30 days, 2018

Atwood, B. J. (2008, October). *The Passion Test.* Retrieved from The Passion Test: http://www.thepassiontest.com

Brittanica.com. (2013). *Science/Diaphragm-Anatomy.* Retrieved from Britannica: https://www.britinnica.com/science/diaphragm-anatomy

Cartlett, M. (2015, December 2). *21 Mantras for Meditation.* Retrieved from Programminglife.net http://programminglife.net/mantras-for-meditation

Chambers, T. (2014). *The Sage Within.* Negril, Jamaica, W.I.: Temple of Inner Peace.

Chopra, D. (2018). *The Law of Least Effort.* Retrieved from The Chopra Center: http://chopra.com/articles/the-law-of-least-effort

Cok Sui, C. M. (2017). Twin Hearts Meditation [Recorded by S. M. Co].

Dyer, W. (1997). *Manifest Your Destiny.* New York: HarperCollins.

Dyer, W. D. (n.d.). *Daily Inspiration Quotes.* Retrieved from drwaynedyer. com: https://www.drwaynedyer.com/wayne-dyer-quotes/

Gibran, K. (1923). Coming of the Ship. In K. Gibran, *The Prophet.* New York, NY: Alfred A. Knopf Inc.

Helmstetter, S. D. (2017). *What to Say When you Talk to Yourself.* New York: Simon & Schuster.

Janki, D. (2003). *Inside Out.* London: Brahma Kumaris Publications.

King, M. L. (1963, August 28). *I Have a Dream Speech.* Retrieved from www. YouTube.com: https://www.youtube.com/watch?v=3vDWWy4CMhE

Lakhiani, V. (n.d.). *Root Chakra - Guide to Heath Balance*. Retrieved from Mindvalley: https://blog.mindvalley.com/root-chakra/

Paine, T. (1776). *American Crisis*. Great Britain: Self-Published.

Parris-Chambers, S. (2011). *Poetry From the Rose: Divine Thoughts for Living Well*. South Carolina: Temple of Inner Peace.

Sebastian, S. (2018). *Chakra Anatomy*. Retrieved from Chakra-Anatomy.com: www.chakra-anatomy.com/root-chakra-colors.html

Sharma, R. (2007). *The Monk who Sold his Ferrari*. Toronto: Harper Collins.

Tandon, C. (2015). *Ancient Wisdom in Modern Times - Deepak Chopra & Sadhguru*. Retrieved from Youtube.com: https://www.Youtube.com/watch?v=WMhJgdpj1d0

TheBuddahfultao.com. (2012, January 29). Retrieved from TheBuddhafultao.com/Some great koans: https://thebuddhafultao.wordpress.com

Tillman, D. (2001). *Living Values*. Deerfield Beach, Florida: Health Communications, Inc.

Vaughn-Lee, L. (2007). *The Divine Feminine*. Retrieved from Whenthesoulawakens: http://whenthesoulawakens.org/the-divine-feminine_275.html

Williamson, M. (1992). *A Return to Love: Reflections on the Principles of 'A Course in Miracles'*. New York, NY: HarperCollins Publishers, Inc.

Praise For The Book: *Living Life As A Spiritual Practice: Discover Yourself as a Source of Creation*

By Sharon Parris-Chambers

1. Mutabaruka, Poet, Cultural Historian, Journalist & Radio Host

   "Action speaks to the temporary
   It happens then leaves
   We want action
   But we need inspiration to act upon
   Yet words are not just words
   They are what inspire us to take action
   Words create
   Words motivate
   Be motivated
   By these words."

2. Myrtha Desulmè: President of the Haiti-Jamaica Society VP for Advocacy and Public Policy of the Haitian Diaspora Federation.

   "Living Life as a Sacred Practice" is a book disseminating Peace, Love, and Wisdom. It reminds us at every moment of our rightful place in the universe, that we are co-Creators of our reality, and Children of the Almighty."

3. Rachel Citrin, Author & Yogini.

    "Each chapter offers a meditation practice that is simple and easy. It is a practice of joy, our natural state of being. Sharon reinforces the truth, that we are Light beings, spreading light, joy, love, aliveness. We are energy and so much more. Sharon's work is a gift to humanity."
    -Rachel Citrin, Mexico.

4. Gloria Spence, Hotelier & Sociologist.

    "Living Life as a Sacred Practice" is the definitive book on self-discovery. In a time harangued by competitiveness and survival, it beckons us to explore our inner space. Therein, we find the answers to our every concern."

5. Abijah Smith, Reggae Entertainer, Musician & Teacher of One Love.

    "People who ask "why?" keep others from getting things done. Those who ask, "why not?" get things done. Sharon's book: *Living life as a Sacred Practice: Discover yourself as a Source of Creation*. Brilliant! I've known Sharon for years and she get things done, always in One Love."

6. Michael Olotu, Spiritual Teacher

    "Thank you for the affirmative sacred life practice. You don't know how much this piece touches my heart in an unexplainable manner. Anyway, I love the feel, and want you to know that you are more powerful than your wildest imagination. You are eternal spirit, flowing, positive energy, a genius creator manifesting who you really are and why you came here to this planet at this time."

7. Julius Garvey, M.D. Cardiothoracic & Vascular Surgeon

"The search for 'Who am I'? was first recognized & answered in Kemet, our earliest civilization. BEING is PRESENCE and the ability to live within the SOURCE of all LIFE, beyond the birth & death of impermanent forms. Sharon in this work using varied references & techniques has cleared a pathway for us to regain AWARENESS of BEING, rest in that state of feeling/knowing & function optimally in the ordinary day to day world, moment by moment.

Epilogue

My wish for all readers is to advance in spiritual development and to find blissfulness in your life through positive life experiences. I encourage you to use *Living Life as a Sacred Practice: Discover Yourself as a Source of Creation* as a self-help tool on your journey.

There is a point where we move from Mindfullness to Breathfullness and Breathdancing™, a term used by myself and Desmond Green, founder of Reverence for Life Foundation.

The focus here is on the breath as your life source Chi or Prana. When the breath is flowing effortlessly without blockages, the being is aligned with the universe. Following the breath allows an effortless flow into the meditative state. Learning qigong or other forms of energy practices, teach how to keep the breath flowing through movements and meditative postures which sustains and enhances the body both spiritually and physically.

BREATHFULLNESS

Breathfullness is a oneness with the breath. The breath is one's constitution for living. Where would you be without your breath?

Empty the mind and focus on the breath. Enjoy the freedom of existing outside the confines of the mind and discover your Divine self.

Breathdancing ™ is using the breath to sustain the body, removing blockages with forceful breathing, movement and recognition that you are your breath. Awareness of the breath informs the quality of your life. Conscious breathers have no fear or lack. Their attitude is a magnet for success.

Take a few minutes today to reflect on the environment and your connection to it. The environment, and the earth, is a part of the Divine Universe. Your Breath is your connection to the Divine. The environment is your body and it lives you. You have a responsibility to take care of the environment because it is YOU."

Chi or Prana is universal breath consciousness. You connect to it through deep breathing, through your meditations, through your thoughts & INTENSIONS. Take in life energy and exhale unwanted feelings, the more life energy you take in, the more positive, and healthy you become.

You may receive Chi or Prana energy through hands-on application of Reiki healing, Pranic healing and other forms of energy healing. Holistic Massage is also a healing system that can harness and apply Chi energy for relaxation and wellbeing.

Breathfullness Practice & Chorus
by *Desmond Green:

Eye love my breath as me, Eye love my Breath as you,

Eye love my Breath as me and you, Eye do, Eye do, Eye do!!
Eye trust my breath as me, Eye trust my Breath as you
Eye trust my Breath as me and you, eye do, eye do,
Eye love and trust my breath as me and you,
Eye love and trust my breath as me and you,
Eye love and trust my Breath as me and you,
Eye do! Eye do! eye Do!!

(2) For eye am my physical Breath now,
Eye am my Physical Breath now,
Eye am my physical breath now,
Eye am and so are you,
Eye am and so are you
Eye am my physical breath now
Eye am my physical breath now
Eye am my Physical Breath now
Eye am and so are you!!

(3) And the more we breathe consciously together, together, together,
Yes, the more we breathe consciously together,
The happier, Healthier, Wealthier, Freer, Wiser, and sweeter we will feel,
For my breath is your Breath, and your breath is my breath,
And the more we breathe consciously together, together, together,
Yes, the more we breathe consciously together,
The Happier, Healthier, Wealthier, Freer, Wiser, and sweeter we will feel,

(4) For eye am, Eye am, eye am, eye am my Breath of Paradise,
Eye am, eye am, eye am, eye am my breath of Paradise,
Eye am, eye am, eye am, eye am, my Breath of Paradise
Yes, eye am, eye am my breath of Paradise!!
You are, you are, you are, you are, your breath of Paradise,
You are you are, you are, you are your breath of Paradise
You are, you are, you are, you are your breath of Paradise
Yes, you are, you are your Breath of Paradise,

We are we are we are, we are our Breath of Paradise,
We are, we are, we are, we are our Breath of Paradise,
We are, we are, we are, we are our Breath of Paradise
Yes, we are, we are, our Breath of Paradise!!

*Desmond Green is founder, Reverence for Life Foundation & Breathfullness thought leader.

During the writing of this book, my search for truth and self-development has led to the discovery of Qisynthesis, a healing modality pioneered by Dr. Glenville Ashby that incorporates Qigong, Psychoanalysis and Mindfulness (breath consciousness). Dr Ashby is the author of "Qisynthesis Journey to a Greater you in 30 days," the foundation book for a distance learning certification course. Subsequently I have taken the course in August 2018 and received certification as a Group Leader. Qisynthesis and its challenge to discover and experience the 'greater you,' my greater self, has propelled me on an amazing journey that began over 20 years ago. I have since become much more aware of my Chi (life source) and how I can direct it for self-healing and the healing of others. This new practice of Qisynthesis has brought to the surface emotions, pain, dis-ease and attitudes to be accepted, cleared and healed. As the Observer and Creator of my life, I have learned to see the ego (Mind) as friend to be harnessed. I see ego as part of the mind, part of consciousness that influences my daily behavior either positively or negatively, based on how I as creator direct my thoughts.

Having received a B.A. degree in Psychology, I recognize this transcultural approach to wellness as most refreshing and timely. The seeker now has diverse tools to unblock repressed thoughts and images through the talking cure (psychoanalysis), movement, breath work (mindfulness) and energy cultivation (qigong). Truly a healing liberating experience.

My wellness consultation practice (Caribbean Wellness Network) offers: Pranic Healing, QiSynthesis, Reiki, Yoga and Wholistic Massage and Wellness Lifestyle Coaching consultation.

Facilitation is available for conferences, retreats and workshops.

Namastè

Contact:
Caribbean Wellness Network
Negril, Jamaica, West Indies
www.Sharon-Chambers.com
Parrischambers@gmail.com
876-275-3169
404-300-9745

Conversations of the Heart
By Sharon Parris-Chambers

My Breath is my beloved; I honor it.

My heart is occupied by my breath.
I am claimed…spoken for.
There is no space for another love.
Loving myself truly inspires me against broken hearts.
I don't barter universal love; I give it freely.
I love myself truly; it's unconditional.
Broken dreams create trauma and drama.
It's time for renewal, to be wholesome and true.
My breath is my beloved.
It is my connection to the Divine.
Excerpt from *Poetry from the Rose of Sharon: Divine Thoughts for Living Well.*

www.ingramcontent.com/pod-product-compliance
Lightning Source LLC
Chambersburg PA
CBHW060050100426
42742CB00014B/2759